GRANNY SQUARES

FRANÇOISE **VAUZEILLES**

Photography by Julie Robert

GRANNY SQUARES

Over **35** simple and original projects for home and wardrobe

GRANNY SQUARES

Introduction

With the return to fashion of all things vintage, the granny square is trendy once again. From being showcased on social media as a perfect symbol of handmade, slow fashion, hobbies at home and recycling, they are everywhere – and never looked cooler.

This easy-to-master crochet technique is ideal to bring some fun to your wardrobe and interiors, particularly when it comes to adding a splash of colour. Go for colourful yarns and play around with bold contrasting colours. With just a crochet hook and a few balls of yarn, you can create your own throws, cushions and decorations as well as jackets, tops, scarves and mittens. Also, the granny square offers the ideal opportunity to use up all the offcuts you have lying around. Even if you have never crocheted before, you can still create these granny square projects. There's a guide to crocheting on page 110, along with a list of the abbreviations and instructions used in this book.

I would love these colourful pages to be a source of creative inspiration for you, just as they were for me each and every day and throughout the seasons as I was writing this book. And I sincerely hope that the hours spent crocheting will allow you, as Walt Disney said, 'to dream your life in colours, as that is the secret of happiness'!

The granny square
These squares, which were crocheted with love by our grandmothers, have come back into fashion. Despite their name, they can be any shape – round, triangular, stars… Whether dark or colourful, small or XXL, regardless of the yarn or hook used, they allow you to create decorations and items of clothing to bring a touch of something different to your wardrobe.

Contents

Tabard 10

Geometric cushion 12

Lavender bag 14

Scarf with tassels 16

Multicoloured cushion 18

Summer pop top 20

Flask cover 22

T-shirt collar 24

Converse with flowers 26

Flowery footrest 28

Bohemian shopping bag 30

Cosy gilet 32

Granny's paperweight 34

Floral shawl 36

Colourful garland 38

Decorative pot cover 40

Turquoise mittens 42

Guest towel 44

Pretty wall decorations 46

Stylish hat 48

Treasure pots 50

Trinket holder 52	 **Knotted collar** 54	 **Straw basket** 56
 **Lampshade** 58	 **Balloon sleeves** 60	 **Cosy slippers** 62
 **Tablet cover** 64	 **1970s hat** 66	 **City bag** 68
 **Tea cosy** 70	 **Open-weave kerchief** 72	 **Soft throw** 74

Bobble hood 76

Floral elbow patches 78

Belt 80

Templates & patterns 84
Crochet techniques 110

Vintage hat 82

GRANNY SQUARES

Tabard

You will need

1 x ball each of DK-weight yarn *(25% worsted wool, 25% acrylic, 50% polyamide – 50g – 125m)* grey, yellow, dark green and blue

1 x ball each of Lace-weight yarn *(100% acrylic – 50g – 210m)* bright green, bright orange and bright pink

1 x ball of Aran-weight yarn *(100% wool – 50g – 104m)* sea blue

Hooks and notions

1 × 3mm crochet hook

1 × 3.5mm crochet hook

1 × pair of 3.5mm circular knitting needles

1 × yarn needle

Granny square

Light square (page 96)

Dimensions

11 × 11cm per square

Front and back
Make 4 light squares with 3mm crochet hook following the pattern on page 96. Using sea blue yarn and 3.5mm hook, add an additional row. Fasten off, weaving in the ends on the back of your work (page 120) and block the squares (page 121).

Assemble the squares to form a large square. Working around the 4 central squares alternating all of the colours (using 3.5mm crochet hook for the sea blue thread) do 16 rounds of:

3 trebles (US doubles), 1 chain stitch in each space and *3 trebles (US doubles), 2 chain stitches, 3 trebles (US doubles)* on each corner.

Front neckline
Make 11 rows of doubles (US singles) at the top of the front piece on each side: 33 doubles (US singles) on the 1st row, reduce by 1 stitch on each side row on the neckline alternating all of the colours, except for the marine blue = 23 doubles (US singles) for each shoulder on the 11th row and 51cm high.

Back neckline
Make 11 rows of doubles (US singles) at the top of the rear across the entire width alternating the colours as with the shoulders on the front = 51cm high.

Finishing touches
Sew the shoulders.

Sew the sides leaving a 23cm opening for the armholes.

Using 3.5mm circular knitting needles and the sea blue yarn, pick up 124 knit stitches for the neckline. Work 5 rows of 2/2 rib. Fasten off the stitches on the front.

For each armhole, pick up 88 knit stitches, work 5 rows of 2/2 rib. Fasten off the stitches on the front.

GRANNY SQUARES

Geometric cushion

You will need

Front cushion cover
1 x ball each of DK-weight yarn *(100% wool – 50g – 125m)* in 8 different colours

Rear cushion cover
1 x ball of yarn DK-weight (100% cotton – 50g – 110m) in a colour matching one of the colours on the front of the cushion

Hooks and notions

1 × 2.5mm crochet hook

1 x yarn needle

1 x sewing needle

1 x cushion 30 x 30cm

1 x roll of thread

Granny squares

Rhubarb square (page 89)
Granny square (page 87)

Dimensions

30 × 30cm per square

Cushion front
Make a rhubarb square with 19 rounds following the pattern on page 89. Work 1 double (US single) in each stitch on the square and join with a slip stitch in top of 1st stitch. Fasten off. Weave in ends on the back of the work (page 120) and block the square (page 121).

Cushion back
Make a granny square with 15 rows following the pattern on page 87 and extending with 3 trebles (US doubles) on each side on each round. Work 1 row of doubles (US singles) in each stitch on the square and join with a slip stitch in top of 1st stitch. Fasten off. Weave in ends on the back of the work (page 120) and block the square (page 121).

Assembling
Hold the 2 squares together right side together, attaching on 3 sides. Turn the cover right-side out and insert a fabric-covered cushion that matches one of the colours of the granny squares (this will give you a pretty finish as you will be able to see the cushion through the holes in the granny squares) and sew closed the final side.

Cushion for all occasions
The cushion will sit wonderfully among other cushions and, by playing with materials (one side wool, one side cotton), you will have two cushions in one and can rotate to match the changing seasons.

GRANNY SQUARES

Lavender bag

You will need
1 x ball each of Aran-weight yarn *(100% cotton – 50g – 85m)* coral, strawberry and kiwi

Hooks and notions
1 x 2.5mm crochet hook

1 x yarn needle

1 x small linen or cotton bag filled with lavender 8 x 8cm

Granny square
Cornflower (page 91)

Dimensions
8 × 8cm per square

Squares
Make 2 cornflowers following the pattern on page 91. Fasten off, weaving in the ends on the back of your work (page 120) and block the squares (page 121).

Assembling
Place the two squares right-side together and sew together, but do not forget to slide a small lavender bag inside before sewing closed the final side.

GRANNY SQUARES

Scarf with tassels

You will need
Balls of DK-weight yarn
(100% wool – 50g – 120m)
in bright colours

Hooks and notions
1 x 2.5mm crochet hook

1 x yarn needle

Granny square
Thistle square (page 104)

Dimensions
9.5 × 9.5cm per square

Scarf
Make as many granny squares as you wish to achieve the desired dimensions for your scarf, following the pattern on page 104. Fasten off, weaving in the ends on the back of your work (page 120) and block the squares (page 121).

Form a long rectangle with your squares, and sew together. Attach tassels to the ends. Weave in your ends on the back of your work (page 120).

Tassels
The tassels bring a little something extra to this scarf. To make these, cut out a rectangle of cardboard the same size as you want your tassels. Wrap the yarn 8 times around the cardboard and cut at one of the ends. Insert the hook into a stitch on the end of the scarf, draw the loop of the tassels through the scarf using the hook, insert the tassels into the loop and pull to tighten the tassels onto the scarf.

Tip
This creation is ideal to use up any offcuts of yarn since each granny square only needs around 6g of yarn. It can also be made over time, during breaks or when you have a few quiet moments for yourself.

My first shawl
For me, this project has a strong tie to a particular memory, namely that of my first baby shawl made by my grandmother. The black base, which clearly shows off the bright primary colours, is symbolic of the spirit of granny squares from the 1970s. Just a few years ago, Jean Paul Gaultier brought this back centre stage in one of his winter collections.

GRANNY SQUARES

Multicoloured cushion

You will need

2 x balls of Aran-weight yarn (100% cotton – 50g – 85m) ecru for the base colour and 12 leftover pieces of yarn in rusty brown, pine green, brick red, sea blue, light grey-blue, coral, aubergine, mustard yellow, pink, khaki, pastel pink and grey-green

Hooks and notions

1 x 2.5mm crochet hook

1 x yarn needle

1 x sewing needle

1 x spool of sewing thread

1 x 40 x 40cm of fabric for the back of the cushion

1 x cushion 35 x 35cm

Granny square

Granny square (page 87)

Dimensions

9.5 × 9.5cm per square

Cushion squares
Make 9 granny squares following the pattern on page 87 and completing the 4th row of each square using the ecru colour. Still using the ecru colour, work 1 double (US single) into each stitch on the squares. Fasten off, weaving in the ends on the back of your work (page 120) and block the squares (page 121).

Assembling
Assemble 3 rows of 3 squares using the ecru yarn, hold your squares wrong-side together using a double (US single) to attach together (page 122). Then assemble these 3 rows together to form a large square.

Using the ecru yarn, work 1 double (US single) into the top of each stitch, then work 1 treble (US double) in each stitch, then work 2 rows of 1 double (US single) in each stitch and 2 rows of doubles (US singles) in each stitch around. Join with a slip stitch into the top of the 1st stitch. Weave in your ends on the back of your work (page 121).

Place the fabric for the back and crocheted front right-sides together, and sew together across three of the sides. Turn the cushion cover right-side out and insert the cushion. Sew up the last side.

This cushion is ideal for using up offcuts of yarn.

GRANNY SQUARES

Summer pop top

You will need

1 x ball each of DK-weight yarn (100% cotton – 50g – 120m) clementine, strawberry, raspberry and lychee

2 x balls of DK-weight yarn (100% cotton – 50g – 120m) banana

Hooks and notions

1 x 2.2mm crochet hook

1 x yarn needle

Granny squares

Granny square (page 87)

Dimensions

Granny square + 1 row: 9 x 9cm per square

Mini granny square + 2 rows: 4.5 x 4.5cm per square

The body
Make 20 granny squares with the pink and orange yarn, following the pattern on page 87 and varying the order of the colours. Work the 5th round in the yellow colour on all squares. Weave in your ends on the back of your work (page 120) and block the granny squares (page 121).

Assemble the granny squares to form a 2 x 10 rectangle. Fold the rectangle in half lengthways, right-sides together and sew the side to form a body. Turn right-side out.

Make 20 mini granny squares each 2 rows following the pattern on page 107, using the yellow yarn for the 2nd round. Weave in your ends on the back of your work (page 120) and block the mini granny squares (page 121).

Attach them together to form a long strip, sew this strip to the bottom of the body (2 mini granny squares beneath each larger granny square) and close off the side.

At the top of the body, using the strawberry yarn, work 1 double (US single) in each stitch. Join with a slip stitch into the top of the 1st stitch.

The straps (Make 2)
Make 8 2-round mini granny squares using the yellow yarn for the 2nd row. Fasten off, weave in your ends on the back of your work (page 120) and block the mini granny squares (page 121). Sew them together to form an 8 x 1 strip. Using the strawberry yarn work 1 double (US single) in each stitch along the long edges.

Sew the straps onto the back and front of the top.

Tip
The size of this template can be easily adapted by adding or removing one or more granny squares from the width of the top. Simply add or remove 2 mini granny squares for each larger square. However, don't forget that the granny squares, once assembled, are still extendible to the create the correct sizing..

GRANNY SQUARES

Flask cover

You will need

1 x ball each of DK-weight yarn (100% cotton – 50g – 110m) blue, cream and terracotta

Hooks and notions

1 x 2.5mm crochet hook

1 x yarn needle

1 x 8 x 15cm high flask

Granny squares

Daisy square (page 99)

Daisy wheel (page 92)

Dimensions

8 × 8cm per square

The sides

Make 4 daisy squares following the pattern on page 99.

Using the cream yarn, work the following starting on a corner: trebles (US doubles) to the first corner; 3 trebles (US doubles), 2 chain stitches and 3 trebles (US doubles) on the other corners. Join with a slip stitch into the top of the 1st stitch to finish.

Using the terracotta yarn, work 1 double (US single) into each stitch around and join with a slip stitch into the top of the 1st stitch. Fasten off, weaving in the ends on the back of your work (page 120) and block the squares (page 121).

The base

For the base of the flask, make a daisy wheel following the pattern on page 92, using the blue yarn for the last row.

Finishing touches

Place the two squares right-sides together, and sew one side together. Attach the two other squares in the same way. Then assemble the two rows to form a tube. Sew the daisy granny square to form the base. Turn right-side out.

For the handle, make 120 chain stitches, work a double (US single) in each chain stitch (skip the 1st chain for your turning chain). Weave in your ends on the back of your work.

Insert the two ends of the handle onto the top of the cover in a space between 2 stitches, opposite each other, and tie a knot.

Then, simply slide your flask into your finished creation!

GRANNY SQUARES

T-shirt collar

You will need

1 x ball each of 4-ply yarn (100% cotton – 100g – 400 m) blue and emerald

1 x ball each of DK-weight yarn (100% cotton – 50g – 110m) in a range of colours

Hooks and notions

1 x 2.5mm crochet hook

1 x 3.5mm crochet hook

1 x yarn needle

1 x spool of sewing thread

1 x V-neck T-shirt

Granny squares

Granny square (page 87)

Picot flower (page 106)

Dimensions

Granny square: 5 x 5cm per square

Picot flower: 4 x 4cm per flower

Motifs

With 2.5mm crochet hook, make 4 blue granny squares and 3 emerald granny squares following the pattern on page 87.

With 3.5mm crochet hook, and the other colours, make 8 picot flowers following the pattern on page 106. Weave in your ends on the back of your work (page 120) and block the granny square (page 121).

Finishing touches

Sew them together alternating a picot flower with a granny square. Place on the neckline with a granny square in the middle of the neckline to form a point. Attach your motifs to the neckline with sewing thread.

Tip

The small picot flowers can be used to customize a jean pocket, cover a large button on a cardigan, or hide a small hole on an item of clothing. You can also attach them to your sneakers' laces or on a wax cotton cord to make a long necklace.

GRANNY SQUARES

Converse with flowers

You will need
1 x ball each of Aran-weight yarn (100% cotton – 50g – 85m) in any colour you wish

Hooks and notions
1 x 2.2mm crochet hook

1 x yarn needle

1 x spool of sewing thread

1 x pair of Converse sneakers

Granny squares
Small bouquet (page 107)

Mandevilla (page 108)

Dimensions
Mandevilla: 4 x 4cm per flower

Small bouquet: 3.5 x 3.5cm per flower

Flowers
Make as many small flowers as you wish following the patterns on pages 107 and 108.

Finishing touches
Weave in your ends on the back of your work (page 121) and sew your designs carefully onto your Converse sneakers.

GRANNY SQUARES

Flowery footrest

You will need
Balls of yarn and/or thread in a range of colours and different weights

Hooks and notions
Crochet hooks to match the size of yarn used

1 x yarn needle

1 x 60cm beanbag

Granny squares
Blue poppy (page 88)

Daisy wheel (page 92)

Dimensions
6–14cm depending on square

Motifs
Make as many granny squares as required to cover the beanbag, playing with the 2 different patterns of granny square (pages 88 and 92), as well as the colours and weight of yarns. Weave in your ends on the back of your work (page 120) and block the granny squares (page 121).

Assembly
Lay out your squares with different points touching. Fasten together with a few stitches at their joins to create a millefiori pattern, which can be attached to the top of your beanbag.

GRANNY SQUARES

Bohemian shopping bag

You will need

1 x ball each of Aran-weight yarn (100% cotton – 50g – 85m) blue, navy blue, khaki and grey-green

1 x ball of Aran-weight yarn (100% cotton – 50g – 85m) dark green for assembly

Hooks and notions

1 x 2.5mm crochet hook

1 x yarn needle

Granny square

Light square (page 96)

Dimensions

9.5 x 9.5cm per square

Bag squares
Make 13 light squares following the pattern on page 96 using a range of colours. Fasten off, weaving in the ends on the back of your work (page 120) and block the squares (page 121). Using dark green yarn, work 1 double (US single) into each stitch around each square.

Assembly
Assemble the squares using the crochet hook (page 122). Place two squares right-sides together, insert the hook through the top of both squares, working 1 double (US single) per stitch. Form two crosses, then add the three squares using the layout guide below.

Handles
Using the dark green yarn, work a double (US single) into each stitch at the top of the bag. Work doubles (US singles) from point A to B, work 70 chains (the first handle), joining B to C. Then work doubles (US singles) from C to D, and then from D to E. Work 70 chains (the second handle) joining E to F, then complete the round working doubles (US singles) from F to A. Work 4 rounds in the colour of your choice of doubles (US singles) working in each stitch and chain around. Join with slip stitch into the top of the 1st stitch. Weave in your ends on the back of your work.

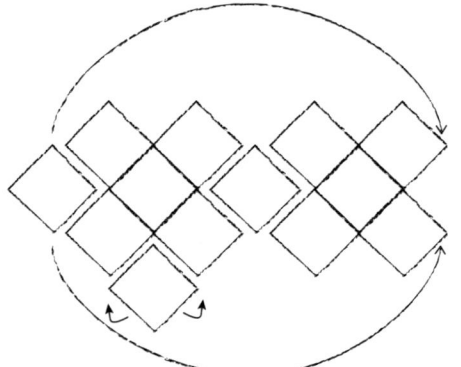

Layout guide

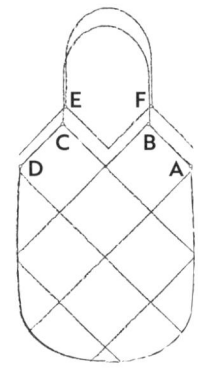

Completed bag

GRANNY SQUARES

Cosy gilet

You will need

8 x balls of Lace-weight yarn (100% mohair – 25g – 175m) in matching colours

4 x balls of Lace-weight yarn (100% mohair – 25g – 175m) ecru

1 x ball of DK-weight yarn (polyester cotton – 150g – 420m) in yellow

1 x ball of DK-weight yarn (polyester cotton – 150g – 420 m) in pearl grey

1 x ball of Lurex (25g – 135 m)

Hooks and notions

1 x 2.5mm crochet hook

1 x yarn needle

Granny square

Granny square (page 87)

Dimensions

14 × 14cm per square

Gilet
Make 24 granny squares following the pattern on page 87, increasing each one by an additional 3 rounds on each square. Use the ecru yarn on the last two rounds. Fasten off, weaving in the ends on the back of your work (page 120) and block the squares (page 121).

Assembly
For the front, create 2 2x3 rectangles. For the back, form 1 4x3 rectangle.

Attach the front and back at the shoulders, stitching together from the edge towards the neckline, leaving the last half a square unworked to form the collar.

Sew together the sides, leaving a gap for your arms.

Make a row of *3 trebles (US doubles), 1 chain stitch* in each space along the bottom of the gilet using the ecru yarn.

Finishing touches
On the neckline/front middle and edges of the sleeves, using the pearl grey yarn, work 1 double (US single) in each stitch around. Then make a row of slip stitches in each stitch with the ecru yarn and Lurex together.

Granny's paperweight

You will need

1 x ball each of DK-weight yarn (100% wool – 50g – 125m) ecru and mustard yellow

1 x ball of gold Lurex

Hooks and notions

1 x 2.5mm crochet hook

1 x 2.2mm crochet hook

1 x yarn needle

1 x medium-sized pebble (approx. 10 x 7cm)

Granny square

Peony (page 98)

Dimensions

5 × 5cm per flower

Pebble covers

Make 1 peony granny square following the pattern on page 98, working only the 1st 2 rounds using the ecru and mustard yellow yarns and 2.5mm crochet hook. Weave in your ends on the back of your work (page 120).

Finishing touches

To enclose your pebble, using the gold Lurex and 2.2mm crochet hook, attach your yarn to any point on the flower, and crochet chains, attaching to other points on the flower with a slip stitch as you work around. Continue to work chains, attaching into the middle of chains with a mixture of half-trebles (US doubles), trebles (US doubles), triple trebles (US doubles) until your pebble is completely enclosed.

GRANNY SQUARES

Floral shawl

You will need

For the shawl
- 5 x balls of DK-weight yarn (100% wool – 50g – 100m) off-white
- 2 x balls of 4-ply-weight yarn (mohair + metallic wire – 35g – 300m) off-white

For the flowers
- A range of colours (around 15g per flower) (100% wool – 50g – 125m)

Hooks and notions

1 x 3.5mm crochet hook

1 x 3mm crochet hook

Granny square

Gerbera (page 102)

Dimensions

Shawl: 70 x 70cm

Flowers: 6.5 x 6.5cm per flower

US terms

tr = dc (double crochet)

The flowers

Holding the yarn and metallic mohair together, crochet 6 chain stitches using 3.5mm crochet hook and close the circle using 1 slip stitch. Then work in rows.

Row 1: 3 ch (counts as 1 tr), 1 ch, 3 tr in the ring, 2 ch, 3 tr in the ring, 1 ch, 1 tr in the ring, 4 ch. Turn the piece around.

Row 2: make 3 tr, 1 ch, 3 tr, 2 ch, 3 tr, 1 ch, 3 tr, 1 ch, 1 tr, 4 ch, turn the piece around.

Repeat row 2 to the end of the yarn.

Shawl squares

Make 15 gerberas in different colours following the pattern on page 102 and working the other wool using 3mm crochet hook. Leave a 30cm yarn tail for attaching.

Weave in your ends on the back of your work (page 120) and block the flowers (page 121).

Finishing touches

Evenly arrange the flowers around the shawl.

For each flower, crochet a small stem with 6 ch and attach the flower to the shawl with a treble crochet.

Weave in your ends on the back of your work.

GRANNY SQUARES

Colourful garland

You will need
12 x balls of Aran-weight yarn (100% cotton – 50g – 85m) in assorted colours
1 x ball of gold Lurex

Hooks and notions
1 x 2.5mm crochet hook
1 x yarn needle

Granny square
Hexagon (page 94)

Dimensions
7.5 x 7.5cm per square

Garland hexagons
Make 20 hexagon granny squares following the pattern on page 94. Using the gold lurex, work a double (US single) into each stitch around. Weave in your ends on the back of your work (page 120) and block the hexagons (page 121).

Assembly
Make a chain 4 metres long and insert this through two holes in each hexagon evenly. Attach the ends and regularly space out the hexagons. Make a small stitch to fix each hexagon onto the garland, if necessary.

Decorative pot cover

You will need

1 x ball each of Super Chunky yarn (100% alpaca – 50g – 33m) ecru, coral, red and garnet

Hooks and notions

1 x 5mm crochet hook

1 x yarn needle

1 x roll of transparent elastic thread

1 x 15 x 15cm pot

Granny square

Dahlia square (page 97)

Dimensions

15 × 15cm per square

Pot squares
Make 3 dahlia squares following the pattern on page 97. Fasten off, weaving in the ends on the back of your work (page 120) and block the squares (page 121).

Assembly
Sew the 3 squares together to form a strip, join the ends of the strip to form a circle.

Work a double (US single) into the top of each stitch of the top and bottom, and join with a slip stitch into the top of the 1st stitch. Weave in your ends on the back of your work (page 120).

Finishing touches
Insert a transparent elastic thread into the bottom row of stitches and attach the ends so as to tighten the base slightly. Slide the pot into the crocheted tube.

Turquoise mittens

You will need

1 x ball of DK-weight yarn (100% wool – 50g – 125m) pigeon blue
1 x ball of turquoise Lurex

Hooks and notions

1 x 3mm crochet hook
1 x 2.5mm crochet hook
1 x pair of 3.75mm circular knitting needles
1 x yarn needle

Granny square

Granny square (page 87)

Dimensions

10.5 x 10.5cm per square

Mittens
For the back of the mittens, make a granny square with 3mm crochet hook, holding the wool and Lurex together, following the pattern on page 87. Do the same for the front, using the wool only. Fasten off, weave in your ends on the back of your work (page 120) and block the squares (page 121).

Assemble the 2 squares by sewing the sides together, leaving an opening for your thumb.

Top edge
At the top of the mittens, using 2.5mm crochet hook and the Lurex, make 1 round of doubles (US singles) inserting the hook into each stitch on the granny squares.

Bottom edge
In the bottom, using 2.5mm crochet hook and the Lurex, make 2 rounds of doubles (US singles) inserting the hook into each row of the squares.

Cuff
Using the circular 3.75mm needles and pigeon blue wool, count up 36 stitches and knit 6.5cm of 3/3 rib. Stop the stitches on the front. Fasten off, weave in your ends on the back of your work.

Make the second mitten identically, leaving an opening for your thumb on the opposite side to the first mitten.

GRANNY SQUARES

Guest towel

You will need
1 x ball each of Aran-weight yarn (100% cotton – 50g – 85m) in your chosen colour

Hooks and notions
1 x 2.5mm crochet hook

1 x yarn needle

Granny square
Trellis square (page 100)

Dimensions
24 × 24cm per square

Trellis square
Make 45 chain stitches. Make 1 trellis square following the pattern on page 100.

Border
On one of the corners of the square, attach your yarn with a slip stitch, make a chain of 20 stitches. Form a loop by attaching into the same corner with a slip stitch. Fasten off, weave your ends into the back of your work (page 120). Block your work (page 121).

GRANNY SQUARES

Pretty wall decorations

You will need

1 x ball each of DK-weight yarn (100% wool – 50g – 125m) pink, brick, red and khaki

Hooks and notions

1 x 2.5mm crochet hook

1 x yarn needle

1 x 18cm embroidery loop

1 x open-weave fabric square

Granny squares

Rhubarb square (page 89)

Triangle (page 93)

Dimensions

Triangle: 5 x 5cm per triangle

Rhubarb square: 5 x 5cm per square

Decoration

Make 1 rhubarb square following the pattern on page 89. Make 8 triangles following the pattern on page 93 with one of the 3 colours of the rhubarb square.

Fasten off, weaving in the ends on the back of your work (page 120) and block the squares and triangles (page 121).

Assembling

To assemble, slide 4 triangles beneath the sides of the square and attach them with a stitch at each end. Slide the other 4 triangles between the 4 previous triangles and attach them with a few stitches to form an 8-petal flower.

Stretch the open-weave fabric or a crocheted square over the loop and attach the flower in the middle.

GRANNY SQUARES

Stylish hat

You will need
1 x ball of DK-weight yarn (100% wool – 50g – 120m) to suit the colour of your hat

Hooks and notions
1 x 2.5mm crochet hook
1 x yarn needle
1 x knitted hat

Granny square
Old rose (page 103)

Dimensions
12 × 12cm per flower

Roses
Make 2 old rose squares following the pattern on page 103. Fasten off, weave in your ends on the back of your work (page 120) and block the roses (page 121).

Cord
Crochet a chain long enough to attach the two roses on the top of the hat. Work 1 double (US single) into each chain, skipping 1 chain at the start for your turning chain.

Assembly
Sew each end to a rose and, sew onto the top of the hat so that the flowers are about 1.5cm from the ears. Sew the flowers onto the hat.

Novel idea
Add some style to that old, forgotten hat at the bottom of your drawer. It will become your favourite seasonal item!

GRANNY SQUARES

Treasure pots

You will need

3 x balls of DK-weight yarn
(100% wool – 50g – 125m)
in contrasting colours

Hooks and notions

1 x 2.5mm crochet hook

1 x yarn needle

1 x 7cm jam jar with a lid
1.5 cm tall

Granny square

Daisy wheel (page 92)

Dimensions

6.5 × 1.5cm per lid

Make 1 daisy wheel granny square following the pattern on page 92.

Work a double (US single) into each stitch and space around your granny square. Make 5 more rounds in the same way. If your lid is thicker or thinner than 1.5cm you can adapt the number of rows to cover it.

For the 7th row, *work 3 doubles (US singles), skip 1 stitch, work 3 doubles (US singles)* repeat this sequence around the entire round. Join with a slip stitch into the top of the 1st stitch. Fasten off and weave in your ends on the back of your work (page 120).

GRANNY SQUARES

Trinket holder

You will need
3 x balls of Super Chunky yarn (100% cotton – 250g – 55m) in matching colours

Hooks and notions
1 x 8mm crochet hook
1 x yarn needle

Granny square
Daisy wheel (page 92)

Dimensions
20cm x 12cm per pot

Main pot
Make 1 daisy wheel granny square following the pattern on page 92, working with the first colour, making the next two rows using the other colours. Join with a slip stitch into the top of the 1st stitch.

Using the primary colour, work 2 doubles (US singles) in each stitch on the granny square and join with slip stitch into the top of the 1st stitch.

Finishing touches
Work a treble (US double) into each stitch from the previous round for 2 rounds. Finish with a row of slip stitches.

Fasten off, weave in your ends at the back of your work (page 120). Work a reverse stitch between the two rows of trebles (US doubles).

GRANNY SQUARES

Knotted collar

You will need
1 x ball each of Super Chunky yarn (100% alpaca – 50g – 33m) ecru, coral, red, garnet and fuchsia

Hooks and notions
1 x 5mm crochet hook
1 x yarn needle

Granny square
Dahlia square (page 97)

Dimensions
22 × 22cm per square

Scarf squares
Make 3 dahlia squares following the pattern on page 97 and completing 2 extra rows. Fasten off, weave in your ends on the back of your work (page 120) and block the squares (page 121).

Shell stitches
Assemble the 3 squares to form a 3 x 1 rectangular strip. Using the fuchsia colour, make a row of shell stitches with 5 trebles (US doubles): attach the yarn to the piece, at a corner, with 1 slip stitch. Work 5 chain stitches and crochet 5 trebles (US doubles) in the 3rd stitch from the slip stitch. *Skip 3 stitches, then crochet 5 trebles (US doubles) in the next stitch*. Repeat the instructions from * to * across the entire outside of the rectangle, making 10 trebles (US doubles) at the corners.

Fasten off, weave in your ends on the back of your work (page 120) and block the piece (page 121).

Finishing touches
Fold the crocheted rectangle in half. At each of the facing ends at the front of the collar, make a chain with 80 chain stitches and crochet a return row with 1 double (US single) in each chain stitch.

These two strings on the collar can be used to tie it to a coat or jacket.

GRANNY SQUARES

Straw basket

You will need
5 x balls of DK-weight yarn (100% cotton – 50g – 110m) in matching colours

Hooks and notions
1 x 2.5mm crochet hook
1 x yarn needle
1 x straw basket

Granny square
Hollyhock (page 95)

Dimensions
9 x 9cm per flower

Flowers
Make 3 hollyhock granny squares following the pattern on page 95. Fasten off, weave in your ends on the back of your work (page 120) and block the squares (page 121).

Sew these flowers onto the basket to form a bouquet.

Additional touch
If you wish, you can stitch stems onto the tip at the front. You can also make more flowers or just one large flower, crocheting this using cotton or a thicker yarn and hook (refer to your ball band for the recommended hook size).

GRANNY SQUARES

Lampshade

You will need
1 x ball each of DK-weight yarn (100% wool – 50g – 125m) light blue and midnight blue

Hooks and notions
1 x 2.5mm crochet hook
1 x yarn needle
1 x 20cm bell-shaped lampshade frame

Granny squares
Triangle (page 93)
Carnation (page 90)

Dimensions
Triangle: 5 x 5cm per triangle
Carnation: 5 x 5cm per square

The lampshade is made up of two sections: a row of triangles for the top and a row of squares for the bottom. These are assembled in a circle, attached to the lampshade frame and stitched together.

Top strip
Make 4 midnight blue triangles and 4 light blue triangles, following the pattern on page 93. Fasten off, weave in your ends on the back of your work (page 120) and block the triangles (page 121).

Stitch the 8 triangles together, alternating the colours. At the bottom of the finished strip, make a light blue double (US single) in each stitch on the triangles, and a row of trebles (US doubles). Finish with a slip stitch. Assemble the triangles at the ends to close the strip in a circle, attach to the top of the frame working a round of 1 double (US single) in each stitch, working around the structure.

Bottom strip
Make 8 identical carnations, following the pattern on page 90. Fasten off, weave in your ends on the back of your work (page 120) and block the squares (page 121).

Stitch the 8 squares together to form an 8 x 1 strip, assemble the squares at the ends to close the circle. Using the light blue yarn, attach these squares to the bottom of the lampshade working a double (US single) in each stitch on the base, working around the structure.

Finishing touches
To finish, stitch the two strips together edge to edge, using the light blue yarn.

GRANNY SQUARES

Balloon sleeves

You will need

3 x balls of Chunky weight yarn (90% virgin wool, 10% polyamide – 100g – 260m) in different colours

1 x ball of Chunky weight yarn (71% alpaca, 25% wool, 4% polyamide – 50g – 140m) in the same colour as the sweater

Hooks and notions

1 x 3mm crochet hook

1 x pair of 3.75mm knitting needles

1 x yarn needle

1 x sweater

Granny square

Granny square (page 87)

Dimensions

14 × 14cm per square

US terms

tr = dc (double crochet)

Make 10 granny squares following the pattern on page 87 and adding an additional row.

Make 2 granny squares: make 4 chains and finish the loop with 1 slip stitch in the base of the chain.

Work in rounds. 3 ch (counts as 1 tr), 1 ch, 3 tr, 2 ch, 3 tr, 1 ch, 3 ch (counts as 1 tr). Turn the piece around.

3 ch to work in the opposite direction. Continue over the next 4 half-rows. Fasten off, weave in your ends on the back of your work (page 120) and block the squares and half-squares (page 121).

Sew the squares in 3 strips from the shoulder to the wrist:

1st and 3rd strips: half granny square + 2 granny squares.

2nd strip: 4 granny squares.

Sew the 3 strips together, by placing the longest in the middle. At the top section, make a row of chain stitches in each stitch on the granny squares to have a clean edge which will make it easier to assemble the sleeve on the body of the sweater. At the wrist, using 3.75mm knitting needles, and the yarn the same colour as the sweater, pick up 32 stitches.

Make the second sleeve in an identical manner.

Unstitch the sleeves from the sweater, or cut them, leaving a little extra. In this latter case, fasten off the knitting stitches with a machine or hand stitch.

Pin the top of the sleeves onto the front of the sweater, around the sleeve line. Assemble the sleeves and sweater using coloured yarn inserting into the double crochet stitches in each of the stitches on the granny squares and sweater at the same time.

Then fold the sleeves in half, right-sides together, and close with double crochet stitches in both edges. Fasten off the wrist with a hand stitch.

GRANNY SQUARES

Cosy slippers

You will need

1 x ball each of Aran-weight yarn (100% cotton – 50g – 85m) ecru, rust brown, curry and lychee

Hooks and notions

1 x 2.5mm crochet hook
1 x yarn needle

Granny square

Granny square (page 87)

Dimensions

UK/US size 5/7.5: 7 × 7cm per square

Slipper squares

Make 7 granny squares following the pattern on page 87. Fasten off, weave in your ends on the back of your work (page 120) and block the squares (page 121).

Assembly

Sew the squares together following the diagram below:

Start with 4 squares (A, B, C, D), to form a diamond, creating the sole and side of the slippers. Add 2 squares (E and F) to the bottom of the diamond (the heel of the slipper), and 1 on the top (G, the top). Attach the sides of E and F, stitch F to B and E to D. Then, stitch the 2 sides of A to the 2 sides of G.

Make the second slipper identically.

The template corresponds to UK/US shoe size 5/7.5. To make a larger or smaller size, count one round more or less when crocheting the squares.

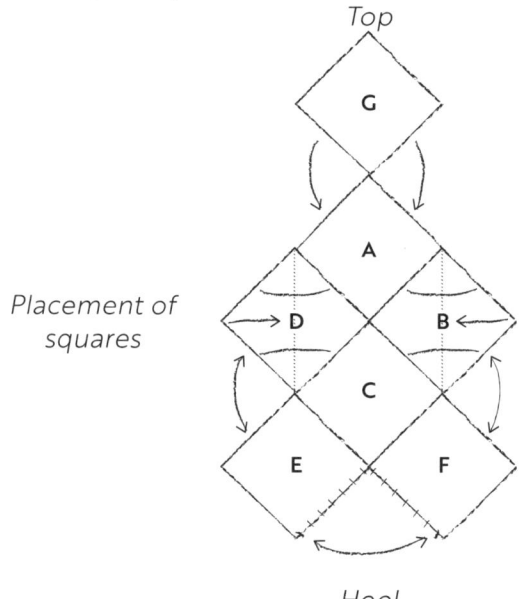

Tablet cover

You will need

1 x ball each of DK-weight yarn (100% cotton – 50g – 110m) ecru (for assembly), denim blue, old pink, rust brown, aubergine, aniseed, khaki, brick, sand and coral

Hooks and notions

1 x 2.5mm crochet hook

Granny square

Light square (page 96)

Dimensions

8 × 8cm per square

The cover

Make 12 light squares, following the pattern on page 96.

Using the ecru yarn, work 1 double (US single) in each stitch around, join with a slip stitch in top of 1st stitch. Fasten off, weave in your ends on the back of your work (page 120) and block the squares (page 121).

Assembly

Place two squares wrong-sides together, and using the ecru yarn join together on one side with a slip stitch in each double (US single), inserting through both squares. Join the three strips of two squares in this way for each side of the cover.

Assemble the front and back of the cover with a row of slip stitches on the sides and bottom of the cover.

Using the ecru yarn, make a row of slip stitches around the opening inserting in each stitch to have a clean edge.

Cord

Using the ecru yarn, make a chain of 150 stitches. Work 1 double in the 2nd chain from your hook, then work a double in each chain. Fasten off and weave in your ends.

Pass the cord through the holes in the squares at the top of the cover.

GRANNY SQUARES

1970s hat

You will need

1 x ball each of 3-ply yarn (100% cotton – 50g – 145m) salmon pink, azalea, saffron and solid white

Hooks and notions

1 x 2.5mm crochet hook
1 x yarn needle

Granny squares

Granny square (page 87)
Light square (page 96)

Dimensions

Light square + 3 rows: 8 x 8cm per square

Granny square: 7 x 7cm per square

Main hat
Make 5 identical light squares adding 3 additional rows following the pattern on page 96. Fasten off, weave in your ends on the back of your work (page 120) and block the squares (page 121).

Join 4 squares to form a 4 x 1 rectangular strip and attach to create a circle. Attach the last square to form the top of the hat.

The brim
Crochet 12 identical granny squares following the pattern on page 87. Fasten off, weave in your ends on the back of your work (page 120) and block the granny squares (page 121). Join them to form a 12 x 1 rectangular strip.

Assembly
Attach the strip to form a circle and stitch at the base of the hat evenly distributed (3 granny squares under each light square).

GRANNY SQUARES

City bag

You will need

1 x ball of Aran-weight yarn (25% wool, 25% acrylic and 50% polyamide – 50g – 68 m) ecru

1 x ball each of Aran-weight yarn (25% wool, 25% acrylic and 50% polyamide – 50g – 68 m) sand and coral

4 x balls of Aran-weight yarn (25% wool, 25% acrylic and 50% polyamide – 50g – 68 m) peacock blue

Hooks and notions

1 x 6mm crochet hook

Granny square

Dahlia square (page 97)

Dimensions

16 × 16cm per square

Bag
Make 5 dahlia squares following the pattern on page 97.

For each square, work 1 double (US single) in each stitch around and join with a slip stitch in the top of 1st stitch. Fasten off.

Stitch a row of 4 squares together, join the ends together to form a circle. Assemble the last square at the bottom as the base of the bag.

Finishing touches
Work 1 double (US single) per stitch around the opening of the bag, making sure to form the handles by making a chain of 10 stitches and skip 10 stitches before resuming the doubles (US singles).

Continue with 3 rows of doubles (US singles) and 1 round of slip stitches. Fasten off, weave in your ends on the back of your work.

GRANNY SQUARES

Tea cosy

You will need
1 x ball each of DK-weight yarn (100% wool – 50g – 125m) cherry, curry, kiwi and strawberry

Hooks and notions
1 x 2.5mm crochet hook
1 x yarn needle
1 x 15cm teapot

Granny square
Trellis square (page 100)

Dimensions
11 × 11cm per square

Trellis squares
Work 2 trellis squares following the pattern on page 100 for 26 stitches and making 4 repetitions of 4 rows in each colour, a total of 16 rows.

On the sides, make 1 row of 2 double (US singles) per treble (US double) using the cherry yarn to have a neat edge, which is easier to assemble. Fasten off, weave in your ends on the back of your work (page 120) and block the squares (page 121).

Assembly
Place the 2 squares wrong-side together and assemble using a double (US single) in each edge stitch, holding both squares at the same time and leaving an opening for the handle and spout.

Slide the cosy over the tea pot. Place a length of yarn in the holes at the penultimate row of the squares, gather together the top of the tea cosy and tie the ends of the yarn together.

Make a 5cm multicoloured or plain pompom with the remaining yarn and attach to the top of the cosy.

GRANNY SQUARES

Open-weave kerchief

You will need
1 x ball each of DK-weight yarn (100% cotton – 50g – 110 m) mauve, aqua green, eucalyptus and denim blue

Hooks and notions
1 x 2.5mm crochet hook
1 x yarn needle

Granny square
Fuchsia flower square (page 105)

Dimensions
10 × 10cm per square

Make 3 fuchsia flower squares following the pattern on page 105, and 3 half-squares.

Half-squares
Draw a diagonal line on the diagram on page 105 and work in rows opposed to rounds: start with the tip, 3 chain stitches at the start of each row (= 1 increase). Using the denim blue, work a round of half-trebles (US half-doubles) around each square and half-square.

Fasten off, weave in your ends on the back of your work (page 120) and block the squares (page 121). Join them together to form a triangle.

Shell stitch
Using the denim blue, crochet a shell stitch on each side of the tip: work 3 chain stitches (counts as 1 treble (US double)), 1 chain stitch, skip 2 stitches, 6 trebles (US doubles) in the same stitch to form a shell, skip 2 stitches, repeat to end.

Strap
At each end, make a chain of 75 chain stitches. Insert the hook into the 2nd stitch from the hook, then work 1 slip stitch in each of the remaining 74 chain stitches.

GRANNY SQUARES

Soft throw

Squares
Make 80 granny squares following the pattern on page 87, using the mustard yellow colour to start and adding a 5th row with ecru around each square. Weave in your ends on the back of your work (page 120) – this will be less tiresome than having to do it once all squares are completed. Block all squares (page 121).

Using ecru yarn, join the squares in 8 x 1 rectangles using a double (US single) in each stitch. Attach the 10 strips together to form a 10 x 8 rectangle.

Border
Once all squares are joined, work 1 round of 3 trebles (US doubles) in each chain space of the squares using the base colour yarn. Using the mustard colour (the centre colour), finish with 2 rounds of doubles (US single), join with a slip stitch into the top of the 1st stitch. Fasten off, weave in your ends on the back of your work.

You will need

9 x balls of DK-weight yarn (50% acrylic and 50% cotton – 50g – 124m) in matching colours

2 x balls of DK-weight yarn (50% acrylic and 50% cotton – 50g – 124m) mustard yellow for the centre of each granny square

6 x balls of DK-weight yarn (50% acrylic and 50% cotton – 50g – 124m) ecru

Hooks and notions
1 x 3.5mm crochet hook

Granny square
Granny square (page 87)

Dimensions
10 × 10cm per square

My memory
This is one of the classic designs of the 1970s. My own personal memory is of one with a black border, bright squares and an ecru centre, which my grandmother made for my cot. This design can be made over the course of several weeks, or even months ... just crochet a square from time to time. It is a wonderful design to use up offcuts of crochet or knitting.

There are no rules, simply combine the colours, take whatever you have to hand, and simply respect one fundamental: choose a base colour, which will highlight the other squares.

GRANNY SQUARES

Bobble hood

You will need

2 x balls each of DK-weight yarn (100% wool – 50g – 110m) red and light pink

1 x ball of DK-weight yarn (100% wool – 50g – 110m) dark pink

Hooks and notions

1 x 3mm crochet hook

1 x yarn needle

Granny square

Orange blossom square (page 101)

Dimensions

7.5 x 7.5cm per square

Hood
Make 32 orange blossom squares following the pattern on page 101. Fasten off, weave in your ends on the back of your work (page 120) and block the squares (page 121).

Join the squares to form a large rectangle of 4 x 8 squares. Fold the rectangle in half and stitch one of the sides to form the base of the hood. Work a row of slip stitches at the bottom of the hood using the dark pink yarn.

Opening
For the opening around the face, using the dark pink yarn, crochet a chain of 65 chain stitches. Then join to hood with a slip stitch in each stitch of the squares around the opening and 65 chain stitches. Make the return row using doubles (US singles).

Finishing touches
Make 2 dark pink pompoms of 6cm in diameter. Stitch these to the ends of both strings.

Stitch the hood around the neckline of your sweatshirt.

GRANNY SQUARES

Floral elbow patches

You will need
1 x ball of Aran-weight yarn (100% cotton – 50g – 85m)

Hooks and notions
1 x 2.5mm crochet hook

1 x yarn needle

1 x ball each of sewing thread in a colour matching the cotton

1 x long-sleeve shirt

Granny square
Old rose (page 103)

Dimensions
12 x 12cm per square

Patches
Make 2 old roses following the pattern on page 103. Fasten off, weave in your ends on the back of your work (page 120) and block the squares (page 121).

Attaching
Stitch the flowers to the shirt sleeves at the elbows using running stitches.

GRANNY SQUARES

Belt

You will need

1 x ball each of Aran-weight yarn (100% cotton – 50g – 85m) blackberry, lemon, almond, strawberry and mint green

Hooks and notions

1 x 2.5mm crochet hook
1 x yarn needle
1 x belt buckle

Granny square

Granny square (page 87)

Dimensions

5 × 5cm per square

Belt
Make 21 granny squares working only 2 rows following the pattern on page 87. Fasten off, weave in your ends on the back of your work (page 120) and block the squares (page 121).

Join the squares together using one of the yarns, making stitches in the corners and along the sides of the squares to make a long strip.

Work 1 round of doubles (US singles) in each stitch and space from the previous round along the long sides of the strip using the same colour yarn you used to sew the squares together. This will give a wonderful clean edge to the belt.

Fix the belt buckle to one of the ends.

Tip
You can either go for a very sober belt buckle, as per our example here, or have some fun in searching out a rare find from the 1970s in a market, second-hand shop or from the bottom of your drawer.

GRANNY SQUARES

Vintage hat

You will need

1 x ball each of Aran-weight yarn (100% virgin wool – 50g – 90 m) terracotta, pearly grey and peacock blue

Hooks and notions

1 x 2.5mm crochet hook

1 x yarn needle

Granny square

Granny square (page 87)

Dimensions

Granny square + 1 row: 8 x 8cm per square

3-round granny square: 6.5 x 6.5cm per square

The hat

Make 7 identical granny squares following the pattern on page 87. Using the blue yarn, add a round of additional trebles (US doubles) in each stitch around the edge of each granny square. Fasten off, weave in your ends on the back of your work (page 120) and block the squares (page 121).

Create a strip of 4 x 1 squares and a strip of 3 x 1 with the middle square at a 45º angle to form a diamond at the centre, with the squares either side of the same corner.

Join the two strips together, pairing the 4 squares to 4 stitchable sides of the 3 squares. Make a row of doubles (US singles) around the face opening.

Make a row of double crochet stitches at the base around the neck line, inserting the hook into one stitch in two on both central squares to reduce the neck size.

Finish with a return row of double crochet stitches to have a neat edge.

The chin strap

Make 7 identical granny squares with 3 rows. Fasten off, weave in your ends on the back of your work (page 120) and block the squares (page 121). Assemble these so as to form a strip. Make 1 round of doubles (US singles) in each stitch around the edges of the strip to form a circle.

Align the top of the chin strap with the bottom of the hat, leaving two granny squares free at the front. Crochet the chin strap and hat together (page 122).

Templates & Patterns

Granny square 87

Blue poppy 88

Rhubarb square 89

Carnation 90

Cornflower 91

Daisy wheel 92

Triangle 93

Hexagon 94

Hollyhock 95

Light square 96

Dahlia 97

TEMPLATES & PATTERNS

Granny square

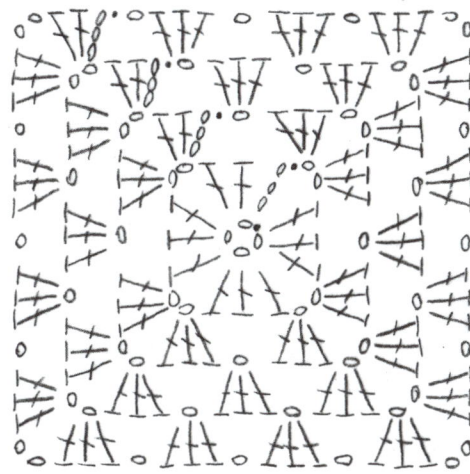

You will need
Yarn (A), (B), (C) and (D)

Stitches
ch st   o

sl st   •

tr   ┬

US Terms
tr = dc (double crochet)

Using yarn A, make 4 ch and fasten off the ring with 1 sl st in 1st ch.

Rnd 1: 3 ch (counts as 1 tr), 2 tr in the middle of the ring, 2 ch. Repeat *3 tr in the middle of the ring, 2 ch* 3 times. Join with a sl st in top of 3 ch. Fasten off.

Rnd 2: Attach yarn B to a corner space, 3 ch (counts as 1 tr), [2 tr, 2 ch, 3 tr] in the same corner. Repeat *1 ch, [3 tr, 2 ch, 3 tr] in the next corner* 3 times. 1 ch, join with a sl st in top of 3 ch. Fasten off.

Rnd 3: Attach yarn C to a corner space, 3 ch (counts as 1 tr), [2 tr, 2 ch, 3 tr] in the same corner. Repeat *1 ch, 3 tr in the next space, 1 ch, [3 tr, 2 ch, 3 tr] in the next corner* 3 times. 1 ch, 3 tr in the next space, 1 ch. Join with a sl st in top of 3 ch. Fasten off.

Rnd 4: Attach yarn D to a corner space, 3 ch (counts as 1 tr), [2 tr, 2 ch, 3 tr] in the same corner-space. Repeat *1 ch, [3 tr, 1 ch] in next 2 chain spaces, [3 tr, 2 ch, 3 tr] in the next corner space* 3 times omitting the last [3 tr, 2 ch, 3 tr]. Join with a sl st in top of 3 ch. Fasten off.

Weave in your ends.

TEMPLATES & PATTERNS

Blue poppy

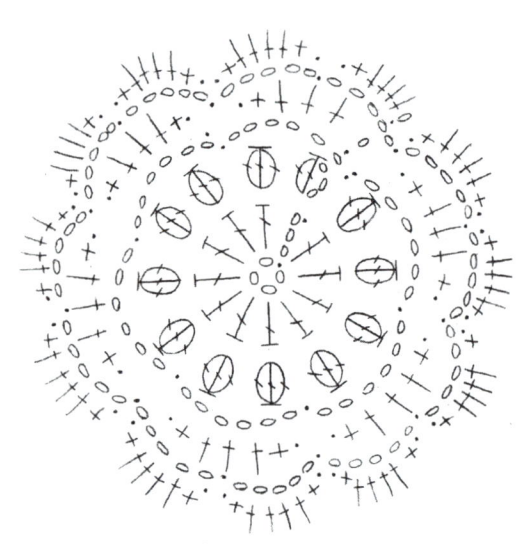

You will need
Yarn (A), (B) and (C)

Stitches
ch st ○

sl st •

dc +

ext dc ┼

tr ┬

3-cluster st

US Terms
dc = sc (single crochet)

ext dc = ext sc (extended single crochet)

With yarn A, make 4 ch and fasten off the ring with 1 sl st in 1st ch.

Rnd 1: 3 ch (counts as 1 tr), 11 tr in the ring, join with a sl st in top of 3 ch. Fasten off.

Rnd 2: Attach yarn B into the top of any st, 3 ch (counts as 1 tr), 1 2-cluster st in the same st, 1 3-cluster st in each st. to the end of the round. Join with a sl st into top of the 1st 3-cluster st.

Rnd 3: Attach yarn C onto one of the space of the ch, repeat *6 ch st, skip 1 space, make 1 sl st in the next space* 6 times.

Rnd 4: 1 sl st in chain space, 1 ch [3 ext dc, 1 dc, 1 sl st] in the same space and 1 sl st in the next space. *[1 sl st, 1 dc, 3 ext dc, 1 dc] in the same space, 1 sl st in the next space* repeat to the end of the round. Fasten off.

Rnd 5: Attach yarn A into the top of any st. between 2 sl st, *make 5 ch st, skip 2 st, make 1 sl st in the next st. (central ext dc), 5 ch st, skip 2 st, make 1 sl st between 2 sl st* repeat to the end of the row.

Rnd 6: 1 sl st in the next chain space, 1 ch, [4 ext dc, 1 dc, 1 sl st] in the same space and 1 sl st in the next chain space. Repeat *[1 dc, 4 ext dc, 1 dc, 1 sl st] in the same chain space, 1 sl st in the next space* 11 times. Fasten off.

Weave in your ends on the back of your work.

TEMPLATES & PATTERNS

Rhubarb square

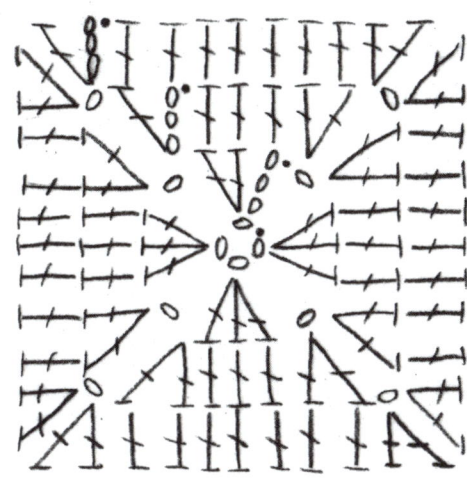

You will need
Yarn (A), (B) and (C)

Stitches
ch st   O
sl st   •
tr   ┬

US Terms
tr = dc (double crochet)

With yarn A, make 4 ch and fasten off the ring with 1 sl st in 1st ch.

Rnd 1: 3 ch (counts as 1 tr), 2 tr in the ring, the [1 ch, 3 tr in the ring] 3 times. 1 ch, join with a sl st in top of 3 ch. Fasten off.

Rnd 2: Attach yarn B to a corner space, 3 ch (counts as 1 tr), [1 tr, 1 ch, 2 tr] in the space. Repeat *1 tr in the next 3 st, [2 tr, 1 ch, 2 tr] in the next corner space* 4 times, omitting the last [2 tr, 1 ch, 2 tr]. Fasten off.

Rnd 3: Attach yarn C to a corner space, 3 ch (counts as 1 tr) and 3 tr in the same corner space. Repeat *1 tr in the next 7 st, 4 tr in the corner* 4 times, omitting the last 4 tr. Fasten off.

Weave in your ends on the back of your work.

TEMPLATES & PATTERNS

Carnation

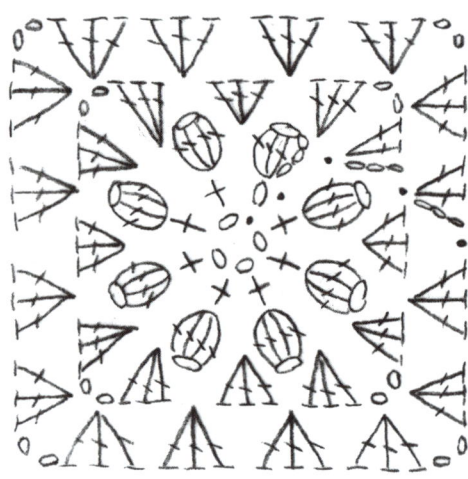

You will need
Yarn (A) and (B)

Stitches
ch st O
sl st •
dc +
tr ┼
popcorn st.

US Terms
dc = sc (single crochet)
tr = dc (double crochet)

With yarn A, make 4 ch and fasten off the ring with 1 sl st in 1st ch.

Rnd 1: 1 ch (counts as 1 dc), 7 dc in the ring and join with sl st into 1st ch.

Rnd 2: 3 ch (counts as 1 tr), 1 popcorn st of 3 tr in the same st, 1 popcorn st of 4 tr in the next 7 st. Make 1 sl st in the starting popcorn st and fasten off.

Rnd 3: Attach yarn B to one of the spaces, 3 ch (counts as 1 tr) and [2 tr, 2 ch, 3 tr] in the same space. Repeat *3 tr in the next space, [3 tr, 2 ch, 3 tr] in the next space* 3 times. 3 tr in the next space and join with sl st into top of 3 ch.

Rnd 4: 3 ch (counts as 1 tr) and 2 tr in the same space. Repeat *[3 tr, 2 ch, 3 tr] in the corner, twice [3 tr in the next space]* 4 times, omitting that last 3 tr. Join with sl st into top of 3 ch. Fasten off.

Weave in your ends on the back of your work.

TEMPLATES & PATTERNS

Cornflower

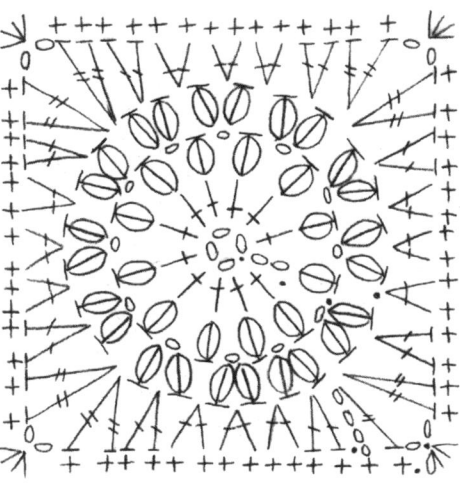

You will need

Yarn (A), (B) and (C)

Stitches

ch st ○

sl st •

ext dc. ┴

dc +

tr ┼

dtr ╪

puff st ◯

US Terms

ext dc = ext sc (extended single crochet)

dtr = tr (treble crochet)

tr = dc (double crochet)

dc = sc (single crochet)

Puff Stitch: *yarn over forming a 1.5cm loop, insert the hook, yarn over and pull up a loop to 1.5cm* repeat 3 times in the same st, yarn over and draw through the 9 loops on the hook. Finish with 1 ch.

With yarn A, make 4 ch and fasten off the ring with 1 sl st in 1st ch.

Rnd 1: 2 ch (counts as 1 ext dc), 11 ext dc in the ring and join with a sl st in top of 2 ch.

Rnd 2: Repeat *1 puff st in 1 ext dc, 1 ch* 12 times. Join with a sl st into top of the 1st puff st and fasten off.

Rnd 3: Attach yarn B into a chain space and make 2 puff st in each space. Join with a sl st into top of the 1st puff st and fasten off.

Rnd 4: Attach yarn C to a chain space above a puff st on the 2nd row, make 4 ch (counts as 1 dtr) and [1 dtr, 2 ch, 2 dtr] in the same space. Repeat *2 tr in the next space, 3 times [2 ext dc in the next space], 2 tr in the next space, [2 dtr, 2 ch, 2 dtr] in the next space* 4 times, omitting the last [2 dtr, 2 ch, 2 dtr]. Join with a sl st into top of 4 ch and fasten off.

Rnd 5: 1 sl st in the corner space, 1 ch (counts as 1 dc) and 3 dc in the same corner. Repeat *1 dc in the next 14 st, 4 dc in the corner* 4 times, omitting the last 4 dc. Join with a sl st into 1st ch, and fasten off.

Weave in your ends on the back of your work.

TEMPLATES & PATTERNS

Daisy wheel

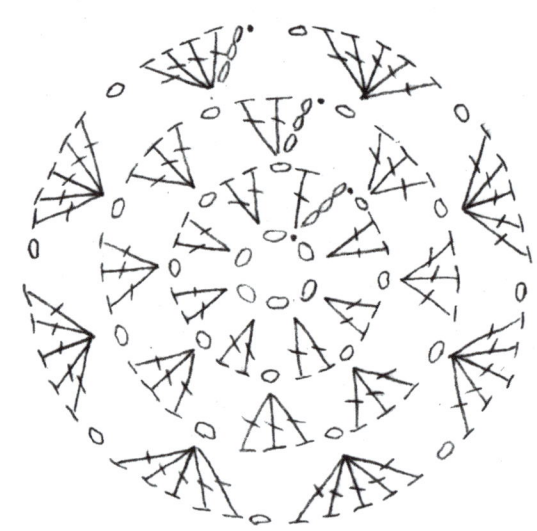

You will need
Yarn (A), (B) and (C)

Stitches
ch st   O
sl st   •
tr   ┬

US Terms
tr = dc (double crochet)

With yarn A, make 6 ch and fasten off the ring with 1 sl st in 1st ch.

Rnd 1: 3 ch (counts as 1 tr), 1 tr in the ring and 1 ch. Repeat *2 tr in the ring, 1 ch* 7 times. Join with a sl st in top of 3 ch. Fasten off.

Rnd 2: Attach yarn B to a chain space, 3 ch (counts as 1 tr), 2 tr in the same space and 1 ch. *3 tr, 1 ch* in the next space, repeat to the end of the round. Join with a sl st in top of 3 ch. Fasten off.

Rnd 3: Attach yarn C to a chain space, 3 ch (counts as 1 tr), 4 tr in the same chain space and 1 ch. *5 tr, 1 ch* in the next chain space, repeat to the end of the round. Join with a sl st in top of 3 ch. Fasten off. Weave in your ends on the back of your work.

TEMPLATES & PATTERNS

Triangle

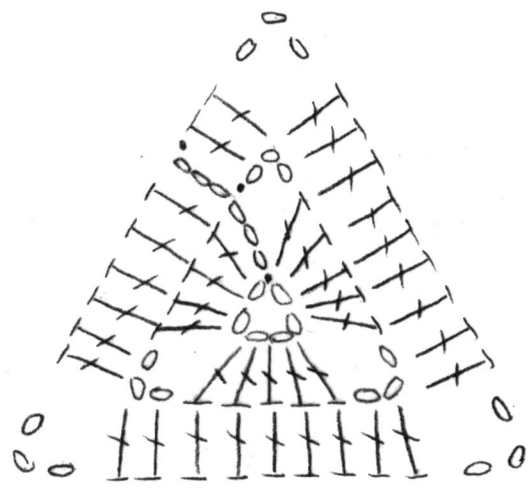

You will need
Use a single yarn

Stitches
ch st O

sl st •

tr †

US Terms
tr = dc (double crochet)

Make 6 ch and fasten off the ring with 1 sl st in 1st ch.

Rnd 1: 3 ch (counts as 1 tr), 4 tr in the ring, 3 ch, [5 tr in the ring, 3 ch] twice. Join with a sl st in top of 3 ch.

Rnd 2: 3 ch (counts as 1 tr) and 1 tr in the next 4 st. Repeat *[2 tr, 3 ch, 2 tr] in the next chain space, 1 tr in the next 5 st* twice. [2 tr, 3 ch, 2 tr] in the next chain space, join with a sl st in top of 3 ch. Fasten off.

Weave in your ends on the back of your work.

TEMPLATES & PATTERNS

Hexagon

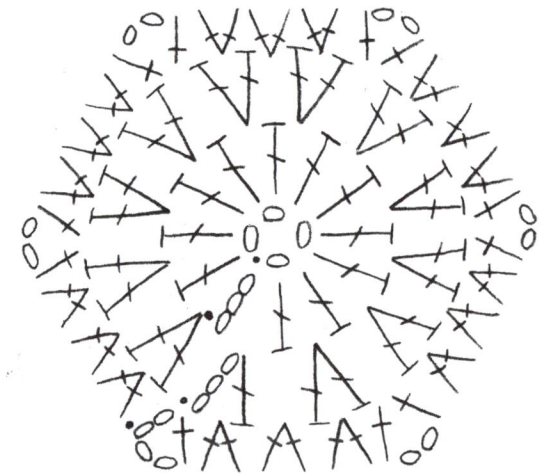

You will need
Yarn (A), (B) and (C)

Stitches
ch st ◯
sl st •
ext dc. ⊥
tr T

US Terms
ext dc = ext sc (extended single crochet)

tr = dc (double crochet)

With yarn A, make 4 ch and fasten off the ring with 1 sl st in 1st ch.

Rnd 1: Using yarn A, 3 ch (counts as 1 tr), 11 tr in the ring, join with a sl st in top of 3 ch. Fasten off.

Rnd 2: Attach yarn B into the top of any st, 3 ch (counts as 1 tr), 1 tr in the same st, 2 tr in the next 11 st, join with a sl st in top of 3 ch. Fasten off.

Rnd 3: Attach yarn C into the top of any st, make 4 ch (counts as 1 ext dc and 2 ch) and 1 ext dc in the same st. Repeat *2 ext dc in the next 3 st, [1 ext dc, 2 ch, 1 ext dc] in the next st* 5 times. 2 ext dc in the next 3 st, Join with a sl st in top of 2 ch and fasten off.

Weave in your ends on the back of your work.

TEMPLATES & PATTERNS

Hollyhock

You will need
Yarn (A) and (B)

Stitches
ch st O
sl st •
dc +
ext dc.
tr
dtr

US Terms
dc = sc (single crochet)
dtr = tr (treble crochet)

With yarn A, 5 ch and fasten off the ring with 1 sl st in 1st ch.

Rnd 1: 2 ch (counts as 1 ext dc), 9 ext dc in the ring and Join with a sl st in top of 2 ch.

Rnd 2: 4 ch (counts as 1 dtr) and 1 dtr in the same st, 2 dtr in each st to the end of the round. Make 1 sl st in the 4th ch from the start and fasten off.

Rnd 3: Attach yarn B into the top of any st, 1 ch (counts as 1 dc), 1 dc in the same st, 2 dc in each st to the end of the round. Join with sl st into top of 4 ch.

Rnd 4: 3 ch, 1 dtr in the same st, [1 dtr, 3 ch, 1 sl st] in the next st. *[1 sl st, 3 ch, 1 dtr] in the next st, [1 dtr, 3 ch, 1 sl st] in the next st* repeat to the end of the round. Fasten off.

Weave in your ends on the back of your work.

TEMPLATES & PATTERNS

Light square

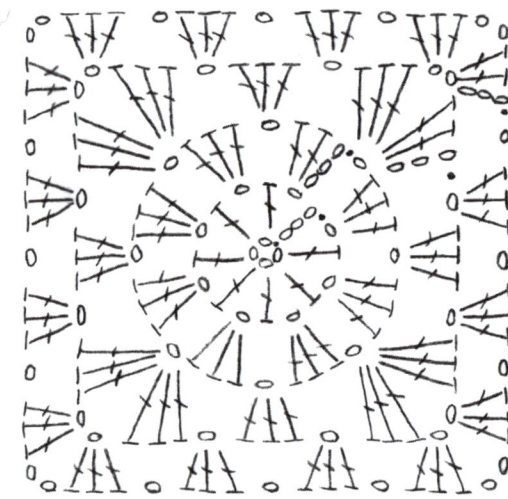

You will need
Yarn (A), (B), (C) and (D)

Stitches
ch st O
sl st •
tr

US Terms
tr = dc (double crochet)

With yarn A make 4 ch and fasten off the ring with 1 sl st in 1st ch.

Rnd 1: 4 ch (counts as 1 tr and 1 ch), repeat *1 tr in the ring, 1 ch* 7 times. Join with a sl st in top of 3 ch. Fasten off.

Rnd 2: Attach yarn B to a chain space, 3 ch (counts as 1 tr) and 2 tr in the same space. Repeat *1 ch, 3 tr in the next space* 7 times. 1 ch, join with a sl st in top of 3 ch. Fasten off.

Rnd 3: Attach yarn C to a chain space, 3 ch (counts as 1 tr), [2 tr, 2 ch, 3 tr] in the same space. Repeat *1 ch, 3 tr in the next space, 1 ch, [3 tr, 2 ch, 3 tr] in the next space* 3 times. 1 ch, 3 tr in the next space, 1 ch. Join with a sl st in top of 3 ch. Fasten off.

Rnd 4: Attach yarn D to a corner space, 3 ch (counts as 1 tr), [2 tr, 2 ch, 3 tr] in the same corner space. Repeat *[1 ch, 3 tr in the next space], 1 ch, [3 tr, 2 ch, 3 tr] in the corner* 4 times omitting the last [3 tr, 2 ch, 3 tr]. Join with a sl st in top of 3 ch. Fasten off.

Weave in your ends on the back of your work.

TEMPLATES & PATTERNS

Dahlia

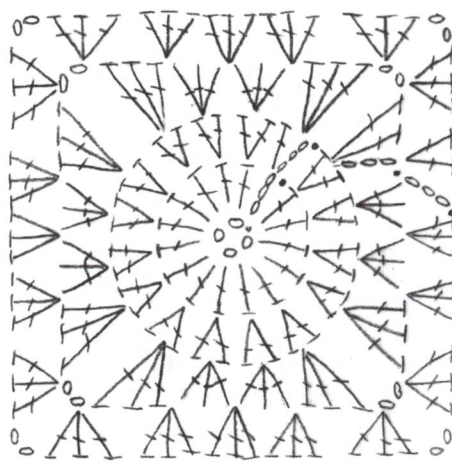

You will need
Yarn (A) and (B)

Stitches
ch st   O

sl st   •

ext dc. ┴

tr   ┬

US Terms
tr = dc (double crochet)

ext dc = ext sc (extended single crochet)

With yarn A, make 4 ch and fasten off the ring with 1 sl st in 1st ch.

Rnd 1: 3 ch (counts as 1 tr), 15 tr in the ring. Join with a sl st in top of 3 ch.

Rnd 2: 3 ch (counts as 1 tr), 1 tr in the same st, 2 tr in each st to the end of the round. Join with a sl st in top of 3 ch. Fasten off.

Rnd 3: Attach yarn B into the top of any st, 3 ch (counts as 1 tr), 2 tr in the same st, 2 ch, skip 1 st, 3 tr in the next st. Repeat *Skip 1 st, [3 ext dc in the next st, skip 1 st] twice, 3tr in the same st, 2 ch, skip 1 st, 3 tr in the same st* 4 times, omitting the last [3 tr, 2 ch, 3 tr]. Join with a sl st in top of 3 ch.

Rnd 4: 3 ch (counts as 1 tr) and 2 tr in the same space. Repeat *[3 tr, 2 ch, 3 tr] in the same corner, 3 times [3 tr in the next space]* 4 times, omitting the last 3 tr. Join with a sl st in top of 3 ch. Fasten off. Weave in your ends on the back of your work.

TEMPLATES & PATTERNS

Peony

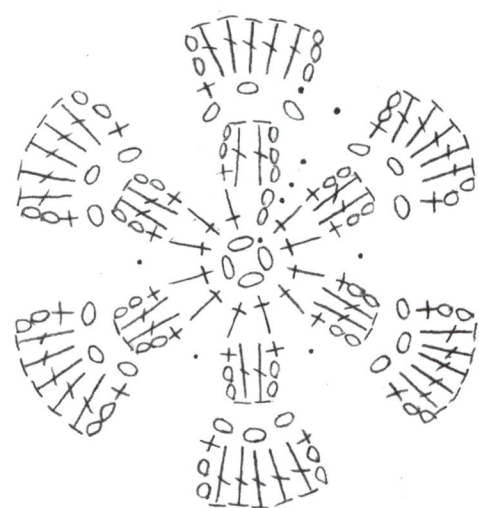

You will need
Yarn (A), (B) and (C)

Stitches
ch st   O

sl st   •

ext dc. ┼

tr   ┬

US Terms
tr = dc (double crochet)

dc = sc (single crochet)

With yarn A, make 4 ch and fasten off the ring with 1 sl st in 1st ch.

Rnd 1: 2 ch (counts as 1 ext dc), 11 ext dc in the ring and join with a sl st in top of 2 ch.

Rnd 2: Attach yarn B into the top of any st. [3 ch, 1 tr] in the same st, [1 tr, 2 ch, 1 dc] in the next st. *[1 dc, 2 ch, 1 tr] in the next st, [1 tr, 2 ch, 1 dc] in the next st* repeat to the end of the round.

Rnd 3: on the reverse of the petal, *3 ch, 1 sl st in the top of any st between 2 petals* repeat to the end of the round.

Rnd 4: Attach yarn C to one of the spaces, [3 ch, 5 tr, 2 ch, 1 dc] in the same space. *[1 dc, 2 ch, 5 tr, 2 ch, 1 dc] in the next space* repeat to the end of the round. Fasten off.

Weave in your ends on the back of your work.

TEMPLATES & PATTERNS

Daisy square

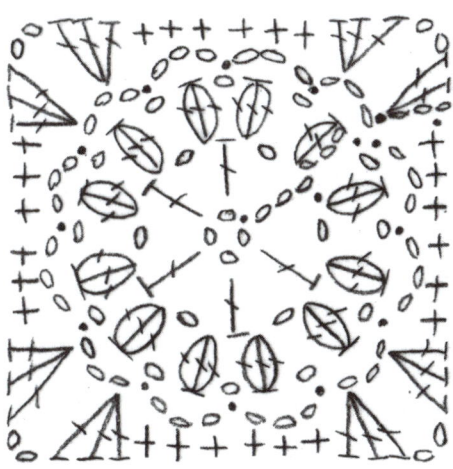

You will need
Yarn (A), (B) and (C)

Stitches
ch st   O

sl st   •

tr   †

ps   ⬭

US Terms
tr = dc (double crochet)

With yarn A, make 4 ch and fasten off the ring with 1 sl st in 1st ch.

Rnd 1: 4 ch (counts as 1 tr and 1 ch), 5 times [1 tr in the ring, 1 ch]. Join with a sl st in top of 3 ch. Fasten off.

Rnd 2: Attach yarn B to a chain space. 3 ch (counts as 1 tr), [1 2-cluster st, 1 ch, 1 2-cluster in the next space, 1 ch. *[1 3-cluster st, 1 ch, 1 3-cluster st] in the next space, 1 ch* repeat to the end of the round. Join in the top of 1st cluster st with 1 sl st and fasten off.

Rnd 3: Attach yarn C to a chain space. *3 ch, 1 sl st in the next space* repeat to the end of the round.

Rnd 4: 1 sl st in the next chain space, 3 ch (counts as 1 tr), [2 tr, 2 ch, 3 tr] in the same space. Repeat *[3 ch in the next space] twice, [3 tr, 2 ch, 3 tr] in the corner* 3 times, omitting the last [3 tr, 2 ch, 3 tr]. Fasten off.

Weave in your ends on the back of your work.

TEMPLATES & PATTERNS

Trellis

You will need
Use a single yarn

Stitches
ch st   O

tr

US Terms
tr = dc (double crochet)

With the yarn, make 21 ch.

Row 1: 2 tr in the 5th ch from the hook (the first 4 ch are counted as 1 tr and 1 ch), Repeat *skip 1 ch, 2 tr in the next ch* 7 times. Skip 1 ch, make 1 tr in the last ch and turn around.

Row 2: 3 ch (counts as 1 tr), skip the first 2 st, Repeat *2 tr in the next space, skip 1 st* 8 times. Tr in the 3rd ch from the start and turn your work.

Repeat row 1-2 until the 8th row and fasten off.

Weave in your ends on the back of your work.

TEMPLATES & PATTERNS

Orange blossom

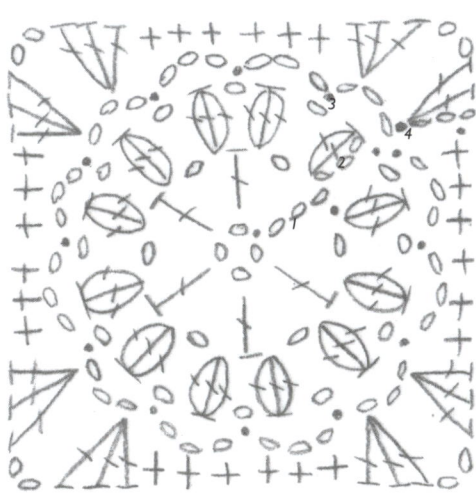

You will need
Yarn (A), (B) and (C)

Stitches

ch st   O

sl st   •

dc   +

tr

3-cluster st

US Terms
tr = dc (double crochet)

With yarn A, make 4 ch and fasten off the ring with 1 sl st in 1st ch.

Rnd 1: 3 ch (counts as 1 tr), *tr, ch, rep 5 times into the ring. Join with a sl st in top of 3 ch.

Rnd 2: Attach yarn B into any ch-sp. 3 ch, *[3-cluster, ch, 3 cluster] into ch-sp, ch, rep from * around. Join with a sl st into the top of 3 ch.

Rnd 3: Attach yarn A into any ch-sp, *ch 3, sl st into next ch-sp, rep from * to end. Last sl st into the 1st 3 ch.

Rnd 4: [3 ch (counts as tr), 2 tr, 2 ch, 3 tr] into same ch-sp. *3 dc into next ch-sp twice, [3 tr, 2 ch, 3 tr] into next ch-sp, rep from * 3 times. 3 dc into next ch-sp twice. Join with a sl st in top of 3 ch. Fasten off.

Weave in your ends on the back of your work.

TEMPLATES & PATTERNS

Gerbera

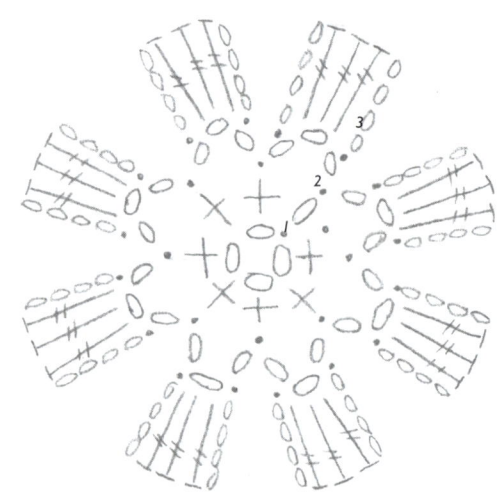

You will need
Yarn (A) and (B)

Stitches
ch st   O
sl st   •
dc   +
dtr   ╪

US Terms
tr = dc (double crochet)

With yarn A, make 4 ch and fasten off the ring with 1 sl st in 1st ch.

Rnd 1: 1 ch (counts as 1 dc), 7 dc in the ring. Join with sl st into 1st ch and fasten off.

Rnd 2: Attach yarn B in the top of any st, *3 ch, 1 dc in the next st* repeat to the end of the round.

Rnd 3: *[1 sl st in the chain space, 4 ch, 3 dtr, 1 sl st] in the same chain space* repeat to the end of the round. Fasten off.

Weave in your ends on the back of your work.

TEMPLATES & PATTERNS

Old rose

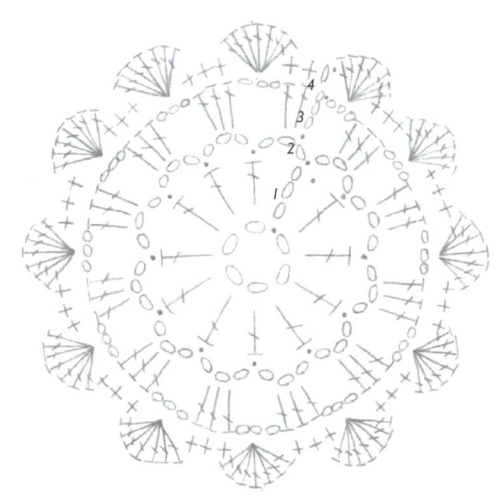

You will need
Use a single yarn

Stitches
ch st O
sl st •
dc +
tr ┼

US Terms
dc = sc (single crochet)

Make 6 ch and fasten off the ring with 1 sl st in 1st ch.

Rnd 1: 3 ch (counts as 1 tr), 11 tr in the ring. Join with a sl st in top of 3 ch.

Rnd 2: *3 ch, 1 sl st in the next st* repeat to the end of the round.

Rnd 3: 1 sl st in the chain space, 3 ch (counts as 1 tr), 2 tr in the same space, 3 ch, *3 tr in the next chain space, 3 ch* repeat to the end of the round. Join with a sl st in top of 3 ch.

Rnd 4: 1 ch (counts as 1 dc), 1 dc in the next 2 st, 7 tr in the chain space, *1 dc in the next 3 st, 7 tr in the chain space* repeat to the end of the round. Join with sl st into 1st ch and fasten off.

Weave in your ends on the back of your work.

TEMPLATES & PATTERNS

Thistle square

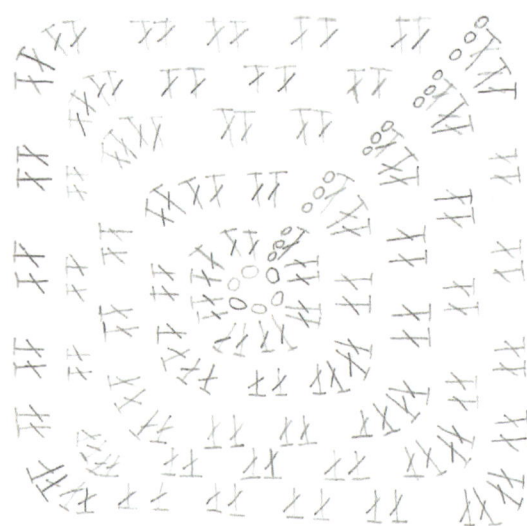

You will need
Yarn (A), (B) and (C)

Stitches
ch st ◯

sl st •

tr †

US Terms
tr = dc (double crochet)

With yarn A, make 6 ch and fasten off the ring with 1 sl st in 1st ch.

Rnd 1: 3 ch (counts as 1 tr), 15 tr in the ring and join with a sl st in top of 3 ch. Fasten off.

Rnd 2: Attach yarn B to a chain space, 3 ch (counts as 1 tr) and 1 tr in the same space. Repeat *1 ch, 2 tr in the same space, 1 ch, 2 tr in the next space* 4 times. 1 ch. Join with a sl st in top of 3 ch. Fasten off.

Rnd 3: Attach yarn B to a chain space, 3 ch (counts as 1 tr) and 1 tr in the same space. Repeat *1 ch, 2 tr in the same space, 1 ch, 2 tr in the next space* 9 times. 1 ch. Join with a sl st in top of 3 ch. Fasten off.

Rnd 4: Attach yarn B to a chain space, 3 ch (counts as 1 tr) and 1 tr in the same space. Repeat *1 ch, 2 tr in the same space, 1 ch, 2 tr in the next space* 13 times. 1 ch. Join with a sl st in top of 3 ch. Fasten off.

Rnd 5: Attach yarn C to a chain space, 3 ch (counts as 1 tr) and 1 tr in the same space. Repeat *1 ch, 2 tr in the same space, 1 ch, 2 tr in the next space* 17 times. 1 ch. Join with a sl st in top of 3 ch. Fasten off.

Weave in your ends on the back of your work.

Fuchsia flower

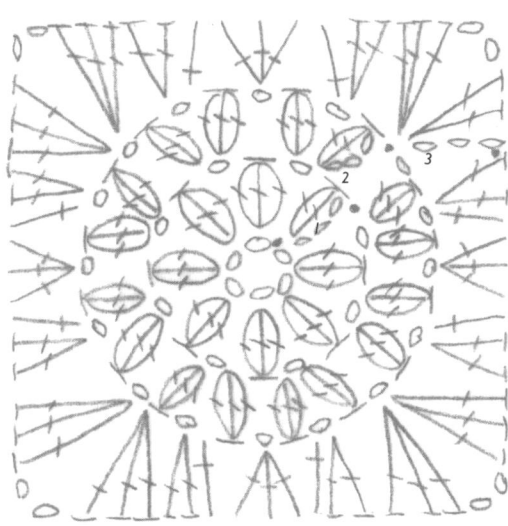

You will need
Yarn (A), (B) and (C)

Stitches
ch st   O
sl st   •
tr |
ext dc. |
2-cluster st
3-cluster st

US Terms
ext dc = ext sc (extended single crochet)

With yarn A, make 6 ch and fasten off the ring with 1 sl st in 1st ch.

Rnd 1: 3 ch (counts as 1 tr), 1 2-cluster st in the ring, 1 ch, Repeat [1 3-cluster st in the ring, 1 ch] 7 times. Join with a sl st in top of 3 ch. Fasten off.

Rnd 2: Attach yarn B to one of the spaces. 3 ch (counts as 1 tr), [1 2-cluster st, 1 ch, 1 3-cluster st] in the same space and 1 ch. *[1 3-cluster st, 1 ch, 1 3-cluster st] in the next space, 1 ch* repeat to the end of the round. Join with a sl st in top of 3 ch. Fasten off.

Rnd 3: Attach yarn C to one of the spaces. 3 ch (counts as 1 tr) and [2 tr, 2 ch, 3 tr] in the same space. Repeat *[2 tr, 1 ext dc] in the next space, 3 ext dc in the next space, [1 ext dc, 2 tr] in the next space, [3 tr, 2 ch, 3 tr] in the next chain space* 3 times, omitting the last [3 tr, 2 ch, 3 tr]. Join with a sl st in top of 3 ch. Fasten off. Weave in your ends on the back of your work.

TEMPLATES & PATTERNS

Picot flower

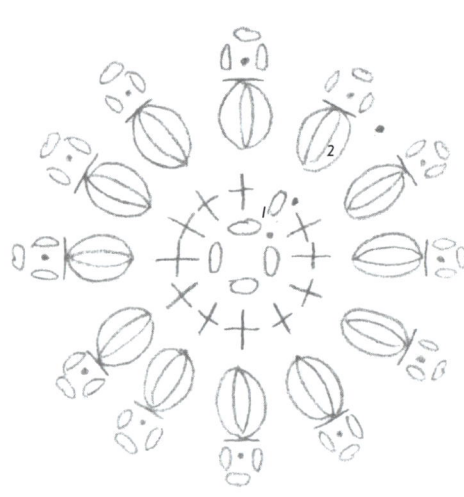

You will need
Yarn (A) and (B)

Stitches
ch st ◯

sl st •

dc +

puff st ⬭

picot st of 3 ch

US Terms
dc = sc (single crochet)

v Stitch: *yarn over forming a 1.5cm loop, insert the hook, yarn over and pull up a loop to 1.5cm* repeat 3 times in the same st, yarn over and draw through the 9 loops on the hook. Finish with 1 ch. With yarn A, 4 ch and fasten off the ring with 1 sl st in 1st ch.

Rnd 1: 1 ch (counts as 1 dc), 11 dc in the ring and join with a sl st into 1st ch.

Rnd 2: Attach yarn B into the top of any st, *1 puff st, 1 picot of 3 ch* repeat in each dc to the end of the round. Join in top of 1st puff stitch with sl st.

Weave in your ends on the back of your work.

TEMPLATES & PATTERNS

Small bouquet

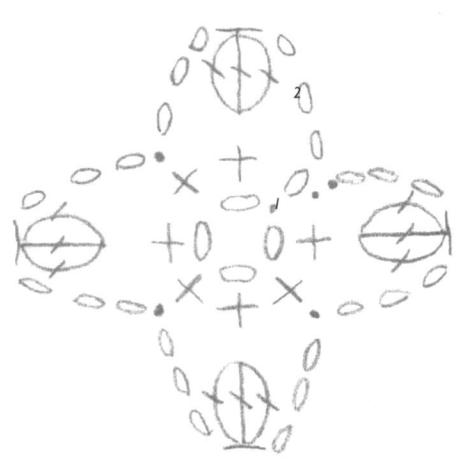

You will need
Yarn (A) and (B)

Stitches
ch st O

sl st •

dc +

puff st ⬭

US Terms
dc = sc (single crochet)

Puff Stitch: *yarn over forming a 1.5cm loop, insert the hook, yarn over and pull up a loop to 1.5cm* repeat 3 times in the same st, yarn over and draw through the 9 loops on the hook. Finish with 1 ch.

With yarn A, make 4 ch and fasten off the ring with 1 sl st in 1st ch.

Rnd 1: 1 ch (counts as 1 dc), 7 dc in the ring. Join with sl st into top of the 1 ch. Fasten off.

Rnd 2: Attach yarn B into the top of any st, *3 ch, 1 puff stitch, 3 ch, 1 sl st* 4 times.

Weave in your ends on the back of your work.

TEMPLATES & PATTERNS

Mandevilla

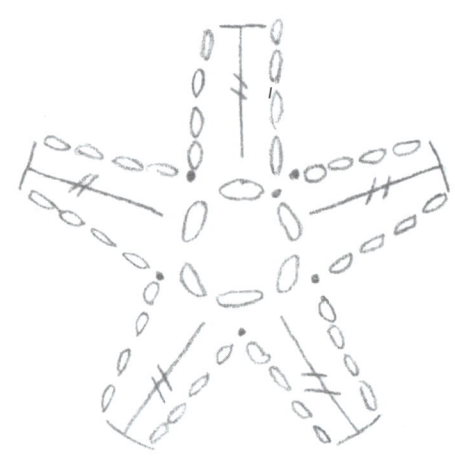

You will need
Use a single yarn

Stitches
ch st   O

sl st   •

dtr   ┼

US Terms
dtr = tr (treble crochet)

Make 6 ch and fasten off the ring with 1 sl st in 1st ch.

Rnd 1: *[4 ch, 1 dtr, 4 ch, 1 sl st] in the ring, repeat 5 times. Fasten off. Weave in your ends on the back of your work.

Crochet techniques

This chapter includes all the handy explanations needed to properly master crochet techniques – the material, abbreviations and symbols, different basic stitches, tips and tricks – and how to crochet different granny squares (squares, shapes and flowers), all of which you will need for the designs in this book.

By varying the yarns and adapting the size of crochet hook or by choosing the hook depending on the design specifications, you will see very different results. For example, for the granny square on page 96, with fine yarn and a 2.5mm crochet hook, you will make a 7cm square (1). With medium-grade cotton and a 3mm crochet hook, the square will measure 9cm (2). Using thick-grade yarn and a 5mm crochet hook the square will measure 12cm (3). With acrylic yarn/thick-grade cotton and a 6mm crochet hook, the square will measure 15cm (4).

CROCHET TECHNIQUES

Here is a list of abbreviations which are used throughout this book. Don't be put off by all the abbreviations, you will soon get used to them.

Asterisks *

Asterisks are used to mark steps which should be repeated. Repeat those steps appearing between asterisks.

Square brackets [ ]

Square brackets indicate a series of stitches which should be repeated or inserted into the same stitch or space.

Brackets ( )

The text appearing between brackets is provided as an explanation. For example: (counts as 1 st).

Table of abbreviations

Stitches used (US terms are in brackets)	Abbreviations (US terms are in brackets)	Symbols
slip stitch	sl st	•
chain stitch	ch	○
double crochet (single crochet)	dc (sc)	+
extended double crochet (extended single crochet)	ext dc (ext sc)	┼
space	sp	
treble crochet (double crochet)	tr (dc)	┼
double treble crochet (treble)	dtr (tr)	┼
2 stitch cluster stitch	2-cluster st	◯
3 stitch cluster stitch	3-cluster st	◯
popcorn stitch	popcorn st	◯

The granny square crochet technique requires very little material: just a pair of scissors (1), a yarn needle, crochets hooks in different sizes (2), and, of course, some yarn (3) in different weights, colours and fibre. Everything and anything can be used to crochet, even string and raffia!

CROCHET TECHNIQUES

Holding the crochet hook

The crochet hook can be handled using the right or left hand. There are typically two ways of holding the crochet hook; use whichever way suits you best.

1. Like a pencil.

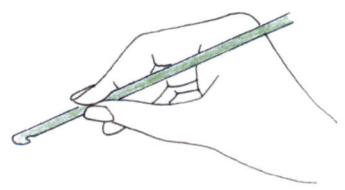

2. Like a knife.

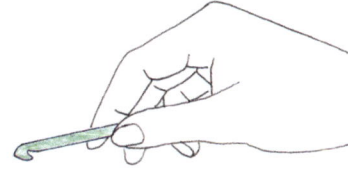

Holding the yarn

The yarn should be held in the hand which is not used to hold the hook. Keep a constant tension on the yarn while crocheting your granny square. There are two methods for this.

Method A

Palm facing upwards, pass the yarn between the ring and little finger, from back to front, wrap around the ring finger and pass it between the ring finger and middle finger. Place it behind the index finger and, bring it across the palm.

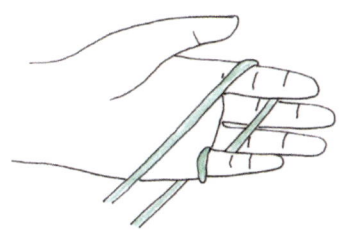

Method B

Pass the yarn over the little finger, palm facing upwards, behind the ring finger, over the middle finger, behind the index finger, and bring it back across the palm.

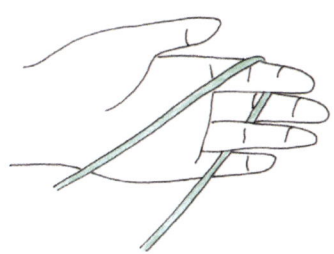

Slip knot

This is how most crochet projects begin.

Always leave enough yarn before creating the loop so once the slip knot is finished, the yarn tail is around 20cm long.

1. Make a loop, with the yarn tail on the right and the ball each of yarn on the left.

2. Pass the crochet hook through the loop, to the right of the end, pass beneath the yarn and pass it through the other side of the yarn, through the loop.

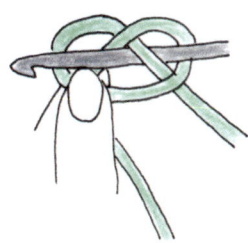

3. Draw on the yarn (from the ball each of yarn) to tighten the loop around the crochet hook. You have now created a slip knot.

CROCHET TECHNIQUES

Chain stitch   ch   ○

1. Make a slip knot. Bring the yarn around the crochet hook, rolling the yarn over the top of the hook towards you (yarn over).

2. Draw the yarn through the loop to form a second loop.

3. Repeat until you have the number of chain stitches required.

Note: to know how many chain stitches you have made, only count those which make up the row, but not the loop which is left on the hook.

Slip stitch   sl st   •

The slip stitch is the simplest crochet stitch. It is used to assemble pieces or end a round.

1. Insert the hook from front to back in the 2nd stitch from the hook.

2. Yarn over and draw through both loops on the hook.

3. The slip stitch is now complete. Repeat until you have the number of slip stitches required.

CROCHET TECHNIQUES

Double crochet   dc   +
(US - Single crochet   sc)

This is a short, firm and clean stitch.

1. Insert the hook from front to back in the 2ⁿᵈ stitch from the hook. Yarn over and draw the yarn through the stitch.

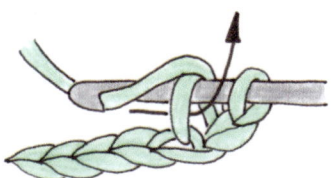

2. Yarn over and draw the yarn through the 2 loops on the hook.

3. You have now completed the double crochet. Repeat until you have the number of doubles (US singles) required.

Extended double crochet   edc   ┼
(US - Extended single crochet   esc)

1. Insert the hook from front to back in the 3ʳᵈ stitch from the hook. Yarn over and draw the yarn through the stitch.

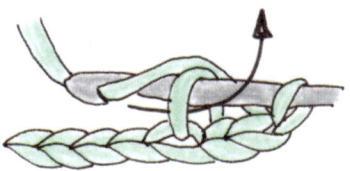

2. Yarn over and draw the yarn through the 1ˢᵗ loop on the hook.

3. Yarn over and draw the yarn through the 2 loops on the hook.

CROCHET TECHNIQUES

Treble crochet   tr (US - Double crochet   dc)

1. Yarn over and insert the hook from front to back in the 4th stitch from the hook.

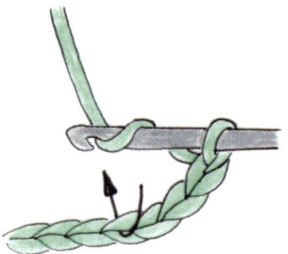

2. Yarn over and draw the yarn through the stitch. A total of 3 loops should be on the hook.

3. Yarn over and draw through the first 2 loops on the hook. 2 loops should be on the hook. Yarn over again and draw the yarn through the 2 loops.

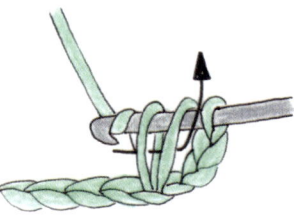

4. The treble is now complete. Repeat until you have the number of trebles (US doubles) required.

Double treble crochet   dtr (US - Triple crochet   tr)

1. Yarn over twice and insert the hook from front to back in the 5th stitch from the hook. Yarn over again and draw the yarn through the stitch. A total of 4 loops should be on the hook.

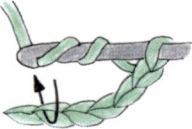

2. Yarn over and draw the yarn through the first 2 loops on the hook. A total of 3 loops should be on the hook.

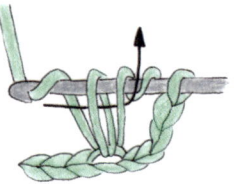

3. Yarn over and draw the yarn through the first 2 loops on the hook. A total of 2 loops should be on the hook.

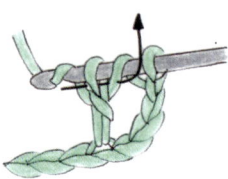

4. Yarn over and draw the yarn through the 2 loops on the hook.

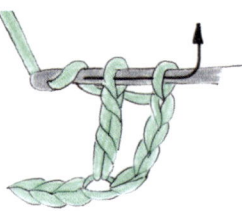

5. The double treble (US triple) is complete. Repeat until you have the required number.

CROCHET TECHNIQUES

Cluster stitch   cluster-st

These stitches comprise at least 3 trebles (US doubles) or double trebles (US triples) inserted through the same stitch and joined at the top by a closing stitch. This example shows you how to create a 3 stitch cluster.

1. Make three trebles (US doubles) stopping before the last step and inserting into the same stitch. Yarn over and draw the yarn through all of the loops.

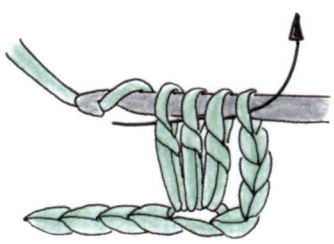

2. Yarn over and fasten off with a chain stitch.

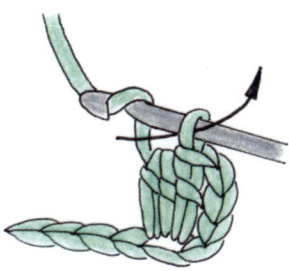

3. The cluster stitch is now complete.

Popcorn stitch   pop st

The popcorn stitch consists of using several trebles (US doubles) or double trebles (US triples) in the same stitch, joining the first and last trebles (US doubles) together at the top.

1. Make the number of trebles (US doubles) indicated always inserting into the same stitch.

2. Pull the crochet through the loop, and insert into the 1st treble, through the last loop and draw the yarn through all of the loops to join them together at the top.

3. The popcorn stitch is now complete. Repeat until you have the number of popcorn stitches required.

CROCHET TECHNIQUES

Changing yarn

There are two techniques to change yarn, whether to begin a new ball each of yarn or to change colour.

Method A

1. At the end of a row or round, fasten off and insert the end of the yarn. Using the new yarn, make a slip knot on the hook and insert into the 1st stitch on the row or round.

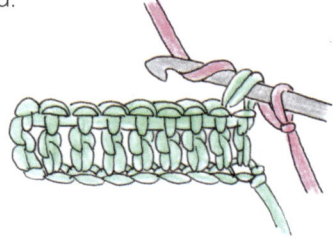

2. Yarn over, make a slip stitch and continue as indicated. When the piece is finished, untie the slip knot and weave in the end of the yarn.

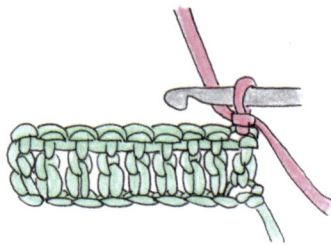

Method B

1. Stop at the final step of the last stitch, so that there are 2 loops left on the hook. Yarn over with the new yarn.

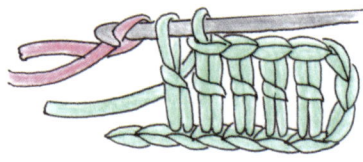

2. Draw the yarn through the 2 loops and continue working with the new yarn.

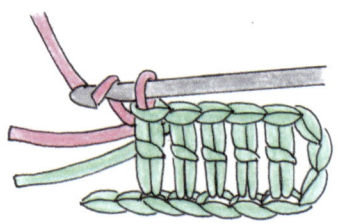

Fasten off and weave in ends

Once the piece is finished, you will need to fasten off the yarn to hold the stitches in place and stop the piece from unravelling.

1. Cut the yarn about 20cm from the hook, yarn over and pull the yarn through the loop. Tighten by gently pulling on the yarn.

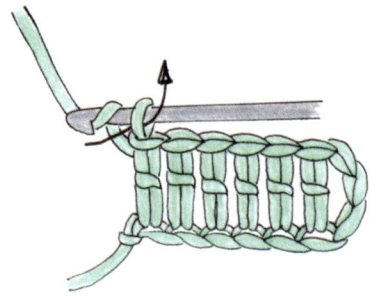

2. Thread a darning needle with the remaining yarn and insert around 8cm of the yarn to the rear of the piece, passing the needle beneath the two loops on each stitch, from bottom to top. Cut off the remaining yarn.

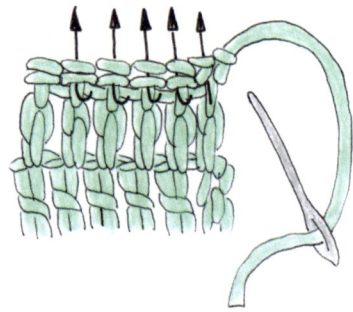

3. Alternatively, thread the yarn tail through the stitches on the wrong side of your creation.

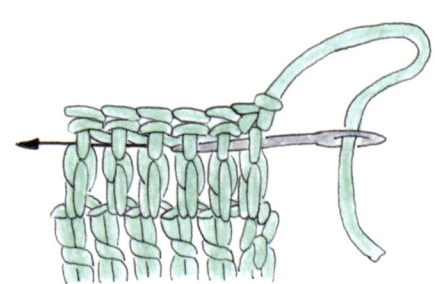

CROCHET TECHNIQUES

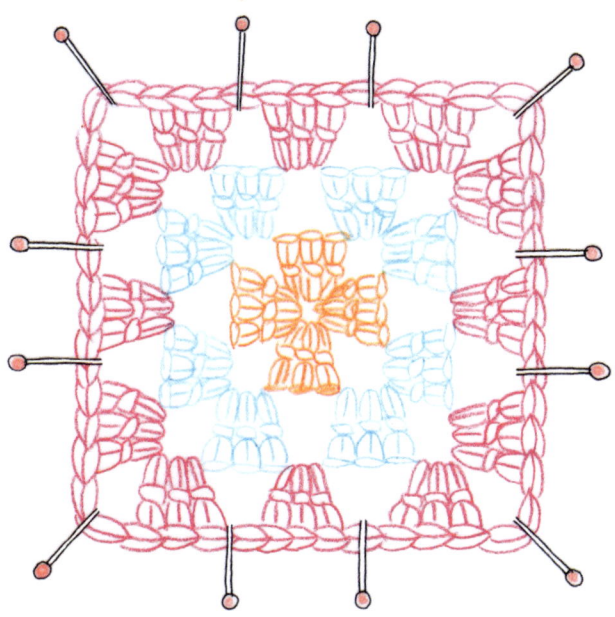

Block a piece

Blocking gives the piece you have just crocheted its final shape and size, while ensuring that the stitches are even. To help you, I suggest making a padded board and tracing squares and circles of different sizes on it using a marker. There are two methods to choose from. Always check the care instructions for the yarn you are using before making your choice.

Method A

This quick and easy method involves passing the finished piece under the steam jet of an iron at a low temperature. Be sure to select the low temperature mode, especially for acrylic or fluffy materials, such as mohair, for example.

1. Lay the project on a stack of towels, padded board, or even an ironing board if you only have a few pieces to block.

2. Pin each piece to the desired size and shape.

3. Hold the iron 3cm above the pieces and let the steam penetrate them. Let them dry completely before removing the pins.

Method B

1. Immerse the item in cold water and squeeze out each piece, without twisting them, so as not to deform them. Place the pieces between two towels and press so the towels absorb as much water as possible.

2. Pin the work to a support and let it dry completely before removing the pins.

Note: Always check your yarn's care instructions before choosing which blocking method you are going to use.

CROCHET TECHNIQUES

Assembling patterns

Sewing together pieces

Carefully line up the stitches and rows of the pieces to be assembled. Hold them in place using pins if necessary. Stitch the pieces together using a sewing needle and thread that is the same colour as the piece, leaving around 10cm at the end.

Running stitch. This gives your work a clean finish. Only insert the needle into the back loop of the stitches (edge to edge and with the back facing you).

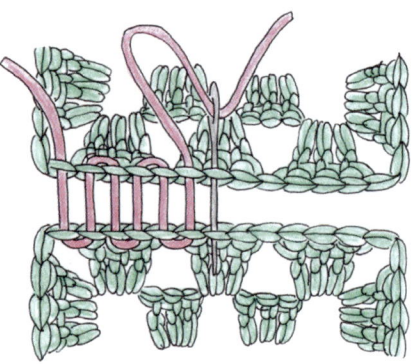

Backstitch. This stitch is very solid (for pieces assembled right-sides together).

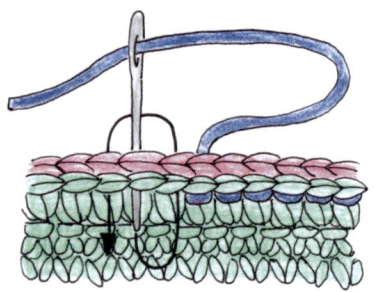

Crocheting together patterns

Attaching pieces with your crochet hook

Always use a crochet hook of the same size and yarn of the same colour as the piece itself. Assembly using double crochet stitches can be undertaken on the front or back of the piece and become an integral part of the pattern itself.

Slip stitches.

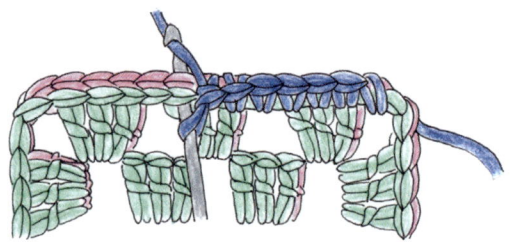

Double (single) crochet.

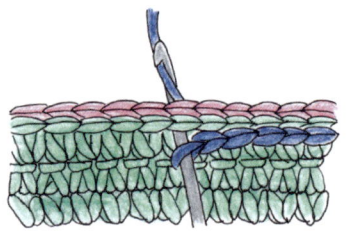

Shell stitches

There are various shell stitches. The number of trebles (US doubles), double trebles (US triples), triple trebles (US double triples) varies depending on the desired effect.

Here the shell stitch is shown on a chain with a total of 4 stitches plus 3 stitches.

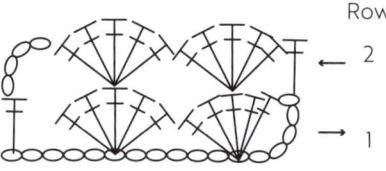

Example with 5 trebles (US doubles)

Row 1 :

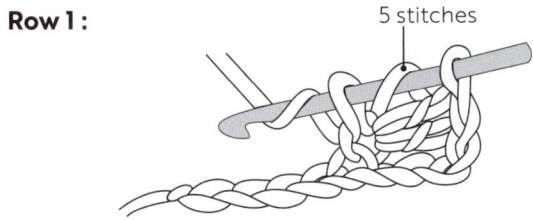

Make 5 trebles (US doubles) in the 5th chain stitch from the hook.

Row 2 :

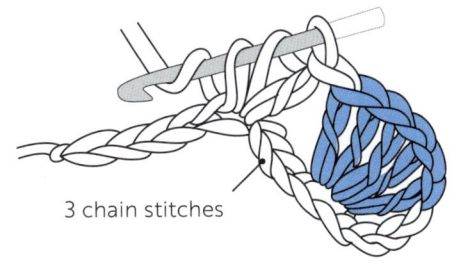

Insert 3 chains, 5 trebles (US doubles) in the next stitch. Repeat across the entire row and finish off with 1 treble inserted into the last chain stitch.

Row 3 :

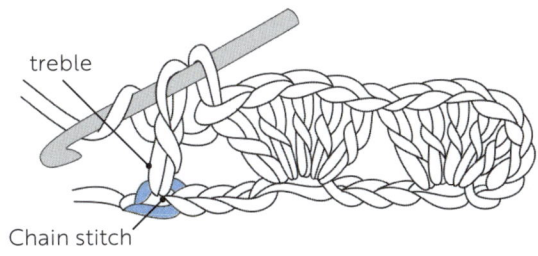

Make 4 chain stitches to turn, *5 trebles (US doubles) in the 3rd loop of the shell stitch from the previous row*, repeat over the entire row and finish with 1 treble (US double) in the 1st chain stitch of the previous row.

Repeat this last row once more.

Acknowledgements

A special word for you Corinne, who always gives so much meaning (and colour) to each of your words while I try to distil a few ideas through my stitches... As children, we dreamed our life in Technicolor; even though it often gave us moments in black and white, we were able to imagine all of these wonderful colours, while never losing sight of the wonderful blue horizon.

Thanks Emma, our wonderful model, for your much cherished and astute participation! You bring such joy and energy to my projects!

Don't throw away your yarn scraps, they can be useful for stuffing amigurumi toys, or many other arty projects.

First published in France in 2022 by Hachette Livre (Marabout) under the title *Pop Crochet*
First published in Great Britain in 2025 by LOM ART, an imprint of Michael O'Mara Books Limited
9 Lion Yard, Tremadoc Road, London SW4 7NQ

EU representative:
Authorised Rep Compliance Ltd, Ground Floor
71 Baggot Street Lower, Dublin D02 P593, Ireland

Copyright © Hachette Livre (Marabout) 2022

All rights reserved. You may not copy, store, distribute, transmit, reproduce or otherwise make available this publication (or any part of it) in any form, or by any means (electronic, digital, optical, mechanical, photocopying, recording, machine readable, text/data mining or otherwise), without the prior written permission of the publisher. Any person who does any unauthorized act in relation to this publication may be liable to criminal prosecution and civil claims for damages.

A CIP catalogue record for this book is available from the British Library.

This product is made of material from well-managed, FSC®-certified forests and other controlled sources. The manufacturing processes conform to the environmental regulations of the country of origin.

For further information about our green policy see www.mombooks.com/about/sustainability-climate-focus

Report any safety issues to product.safety@mombooks.com and see www.mombooks.com/contact/product-safety

ISBN: 978-1-915751-47-8 in paperback print format

1 2 3 4 5 6 7 8 9 10

Designed by Frédéric Voisin
Edited by Dominique Montembault
Printed in China

www.mombooks.com